Transforming Higher Education to Prepare Global Leaders:

Is Higher Education Ready for the Global Perspective of Multicultural Education?

GLORIA AMENY-DIXON, PH.D.

© Copyright 2012

Transforming Higher Education to Prepare Global Leaders: Is Higher Education Ready for the Global Perspective of Multicultural Education?

ISBN 978-0-6155-9158-2
Key concepts: Higher education, multicultural education, global education, global leadership, internationalization

Gloria M. Ameny-Dixon, Ph. D.
Founding President/CEO
Ameny-Dixon Education Group, Inc.
U.S.A.

© Copyright 2012

DEDICATION

This book is dedicated to my family, particularly my husband Melvin and children, Arao, Andrew, Sheila, Joshua and Tyler, whose passions, quests for knowledge and interest in equal rights, national and global issues make my life a very worthy journey.

ACKNOWLEDGMENT

My sincere thanks to my daughter Arao Ameny, Editor-in-Chief of the Muslim Community Report, New York, for the time she took to edit the manuscript for this book.

ABOUT THE AUTHOR

Gloria Ameny-Dixon Ph.D. has been working in higher education for 20 years. She was born in Lira, Uganda in 1961. She received both her Ph.D. and Master of Science degrees from Louisiana State University, Baton Rouge, Louisiana. She also received a Bachelor of Veterinary Medicine degree from Makerere University, Kampala, Uganda. Dr. Ameny-Dixon worked a licensed Veterinarian and coordinated the Uganda Dairy Improvement Project, funded by the United Stated Agency for International Development (USAID), a collaborative project between the Ugandan and United States (U.S.) governments, prior to traveling to the U.S. as a visiting Scientist to LSU School of Veterinary Medicine and prior to pursuing her graduate degrees.

Dr. Ameny-Dixon's experience in higher education comes from twenty-years of service at public, private, minority-serving and predominantly white higher education institutions, where she served in various capacities, including serving as one of the few female visiting Scientists, Biology Instructor, Research and Teaching Associate at Louisiana State University, Assistant Professor, Program Coordinator at the University of Indianapolis, Department Chair, Dean of the School of Mathematics and Sciences, Assistant to the President and Vice President for Assessment and Institutional Effectiveness at Martin University, and Associate V.P. for Planning and Assessment at Central State University.

While at these institutions of higher education, Dr. Ameny-Dixon also served on several university committees in preparation for regional and specialized program accreditations by the Southern Association of Colleges and Schools and the Higher Learning Commission of the North Central Association of Schools and Colleges. She also served on diversity committees for specialized program accreditations under the National Committee for Accreditation of Teacher Education (NCATE) and chaired University Curriculum Committees at three institutions of higher education institutions and served as the Chair of the Assessment Committee and Co-Chair of a Self-Study Committee. Dr. Ameny-Dixon's comprehensive experience in higher education in the U.S. and abroad provides her the ability to speak with authority on issues related to higher education, particularly, curriculum, assessment, accreditation and institutional effectiveness issues. Dr. Ameny-Dixon found during her research and service in higher education, while interacting with students, colleagues and fellow higher education administrators that the gaps and misconceptions held by students and fellow higher educational professionals, regardless of their areas of study or academic expertise, partly originated from their lack of exposure to other cultures. She also found that the numerous events covered in the news and presented on U.S. televisions reinforced stereotypes related to race, ethnicity, and culture. She found that with the exception of students and colleagues in the Colleges of Education, most of her students or colleagues had never heard of multicultural education. Most had never heard about the global perspective of multicultural education or diversity in a formal college setting. Many of her students and colleagues had a very fragmented view of "who they are", and how this awareness affected "how they related with people from other nations" living in their communities or pursing higher education on the same campus.

Dr. Ameny-Dixon has been instrumental in procuring federal and state funded grants to promote student learning and assessment, particularly in Science, Technology, Engineering and Mathematics (STEM) education at the college level. She has also been involved in procuring grants to fund educational enrichment activities for disadvantaged K-12 grade youth. Dr. Ameny-Dixon is the Founding President/CEO of Ameny-Dixon Education Group, Inc., an educational organization which provides mathematics and science tutoring programs and educational resources for disadvantaged youth from all cultural backgrounds.

She has authored several science and multicultural education articles, including "Multicultural Education is More Important Now than Ever: A Global Perspective", which has been cited in numerous books used for first-year student experience programs, such "Your College Experience: Strategies for Success" (9th Editions) by John N. Gardener, A. Jerome Jewler and Betsy O. Barefoot (2011). This article is also referenced in various teacher preparation program publications, such as "Tolerance in teacher education: restructuring the curriculum in a diverse but segregated university classroom" by Watson, Sandy White and Linda Johnson (2006) and in speeches by university Presidents (Slaughter 2004).

PREFACE

In "Transforming Higher Education to Prepare Global Leaders: Is Higher Education Ready for the Global Perspective of Multicultural Education?" Dr. Ameny-Dixon discusses reasons why the global perspectives of multicultural education are more important now in higher education than ever. She argues that if higher education institutions hope to lead their nations to face domestic national as well as global concerns in today's economy, their graduates will need to have 21st century skills. If they want lead the nation in combating unemployment, job outsourcing, problems related to the ecosystem, nuclear weapons, terrorism, human rights, and sustainable energy resources, colleges and universities will need to be transformed by including multicultural and global education in their curricula. Colleges and universities will need to lead the nation by applying the global perspective of multicultural education in order to gain the collaboration and trust of educators working in other regions of the world. As technological advancements continue to make the world "feel smaller", institutions of higher education must adapt to these changes and provide learning and research environments similar to those of global communities.

Colleges and Universities must prepare graduates who are global leaders equipped with the skills, knowledge, attitudes or dispositions needed for the 21st century local and global workforce. They must collaborate with institutions within the state and country where they are located as well as those in other regions of the world to develop practical solutions to issues related to the local and global economy, the ecosystem, nuclear weapons, terrorism, and human rights. Institutions of higher education must assume new roles in order to promote local as well as global leadership.

Dr. Ameny-Dixon provides concrete reasons for transformation of institutions of higher education in the U.S. She also states why the global perspective of multicultural education provides an avenue for the transformation needed in the 21st century. She argues that higher education institutions should serve new roles and become models of local and global communities, in addition to serving as centers of educational excellence, democratic values, human rights, and models for the K-12 schools and communities in which they are located.

Table of Contents

DEDICATION iii

ACKNOWLEDGMENT iv

ABOUT THE AUTHOR... v

PREFACE... ix

CHAPTER 1: WHY TRANSFORMATION OF HIGHER EDUCATION IS NECESSARY.......... 1
Reasons for Immediate Transformation of Higher Education... 4

The Changing Role of Higher Education................... 7

Graduates Must Have 21st Century Skills to Remain Competitive.. 11

CHAPTER 2: WHY THE GLOBAL PERSPECTIVE OF MULTICULTURAL EDUCATION IN HIGHER EDUCATION? 15
Irreversible Change Has Occurred in the 21st Century Economy.. 16

Global Competition and Job Outsourcing 18

Global Citizenship 20

Multicultural Principles to Teaching and Learning 22

Multicultural Education and Internationalization ... 22

CHAPTER 3: KEY FEATURES OF AMERICAN INSTITUTIONS OF HIGHER EDUCATION 25

Types of Higher Education Institutions in the U.S. 27

Governance and Public Policy Issues in Higher Education 28

CHAPTER 4: GLOBAL INTERACTIONS MATTER TODAY MORE THAN EVER 35

The Impact of Technology on Global Interactions 37

The Impact of Global Communication 39

CHAPTER 5: WE LIVE IN GLOBAL COMMUNITIES TODAY 41

Composition of Global Communities 42

College and University Campuses Are Global Communities 45

Goals of the Global Learning Communities 46

CHAPTER 6: WHAT IS MULTICULTURAL EDUCATION? 53

Approaches Used to Promote to Multicultural Education 55

CHAPTER 7: WHY IS MULTICULTURAL EDUCATION MORE IMPORTANT NOW THAN EVER? 57

Table of Contents

Multicultural Education and Diversity as
Accreditation Requirements 60

Accountability for Multicultural Education
in Higher Education 65

Colleges and Universities Become
Models for Academic Excellence 68

Colleges and Universities Are Models
of Multicultural Societies 70

Colleges and Universities Become
Models of Democratic Societies 71

Colleges and Universities Become
Human Right Advocates 72

CHAPTER 8: THE MYTH THAT THE ASSIMILATION PERSPECTIVE PROMOTES DIVERSITY 75

The Conceptual Framework of the
Assimilation Perspective 76

Problems with Assimilation Perspective 77

CHAPTER 9: THE GLOBAL PERSPECTIVE OF MULTICULTURAL EDUCATION 81

The Conceptual Framework for the
Global Perspective 81

Equity Pedagogy 83

Curriculum Reform 85

Teaching Toward Social Justice 86

Multicultural Competence 88

Using the Global Perspective to Develop
Global Leaders 88

Global Perspectives, National and
Global Issues 91

CHAPTER 10: NEW ROLES INSTITUTION OF HIGHER EDUCATION MUST ASSUME TO PREPARE GLOBAL LEADERS 97

As a Global Leader Each Institution of
Higher Education Must Promote
Multicultural and Global Education........................ 98

Assuming the Role of a Communiversity
Each Institution of Higher Education
Should Promote Civic Engagement 101

Assuming the Role of a Pluriversity Each
Institution of Higher Education Should Promote
Global Engagement and Global Leadership.......... 104

New Roles for Colleges and Universities
in the U.S. 106

REFERENCES 111

INDEX 125

LIST OF ILLUSTRATIONS

Figure 1:
Key Social Platforms Resulting from
Advanced Technology 38

Figure 2:
Nationalities of 1,000 people living
in a global Village 43

Figure 3:
Languages of 1,000 people living In a
Global Village 44

Figure 4:
Religions of 1,000 people living in a
Global Village 45

Figure 5:
Approaches to Multicultural Education..........55

Figure 6:
Development of a Core Culture
through the Assimilation Perspective 77

Figure 7:
Development of a Shared Culture
from the Global Perspective........................83

Figure 8:
Using Global Perspectives to Develop
Global Citizens..92

CHAPTER 1

WHY TRANSFORMATION OF HIGHER EDUCATION IS NECESSARY

The American Council on Education, the coordinating body which provides leadership and serves as a unifying voice on key higher education issues in the United States, affirms that the three goals of higher education are:

- To increase human knowledge
- To instruct students in order to prepare them to enter the workforce.
- To prepare global leaders who are equipped to live in a diverse world (ACE, 2007)

While the first two goals are reiterated by most institutions of higher education in their mission statements, the third goal is mentioned only few times by some higher education institutions. They acknowledge the fact that in the 21st century graduates are confronted with issues related to diversity at the local and national levels and in the global workplace. Smith (2009) described the importance of the national and global context for diversity in higher education as follows:

> "The question is not whether we want diversity or whether we should accommodate diversity. Rather, it is to ask instead how we can build diversity into the center of higher education, where it can serve as a facilitator of institutional mission and societal purpose."

The responsibility of preparing college and university graduates who will become global leaders in today's increasingly diverse world will require a transformation in the U.S. higher education system. In these contexts the role that technology plays in the development of inclusive and differentiated higher education programs must be considered.

Many of the leaders at U.S. institutions of higher education have not yet identified ways to tackle the methods to be employed in order to achieve the third goal of preparing global leaders. Identification of the strategies and methods to use are further complicated by the long-held belief that multicultural education is unnecessary in higher education except at colleges and universities with teacher education programs where pre-service teachers need to be exposed to diversity issues. For centuries, responsibility was placed on K-12 school leaders and teachers to address issues related to equal treatment of all students regardless of their cultural background (Banks, 2005). At the same time, higher education institutions were not held to the same accountability standards when it came to multicultural education, inclusion and diversity issues. The myth that diversity issues did not belong in higher education was further confounded by the misconception held by some in higher education who suggested that colleges and universities should only concentrate on academic disciplines without incorporating multicultural or global education issues in the disciplines (Sack & Thiel, 1995).

Today, colleges and universities which hope to prepare global leaders must address national and global issues in the curriculum, among its students, faculty and staff. They must have a global perspective of multicultural education and internationalization as these are the realities which define our era. Institutions of higher education must view movement of people, goods, and ideas among people from different regions of the world as new opportunities to rethink their missions rather viewing these as challenges because the impact of globalization is felt in every circle today including economic, public policy as well as grassroots arenas. Education remains at the center of global change in all these arenas. With accelerating transnational dynamics, if education is left of the equation, the impact of globalization will be of proportions we have never imagined (Suarez-Orozco, & Quin-Hilliard, 2004).

Reasons for Immediate Transformation of Higher Education

The increased urgency for institutions of higher education to find ways to fuel economic growth, prepare graduates who are civic-minded and global citizens requires a thorough understanding of domestic as well as global issues. An understanding of diversity in the domestic, national and global context becomes a powerful agent of change (Smith, 2009). Incorporation of the global perspective of multicultural education in higher education becomes an imperative in higher education now than ever (Ameny-Dixon, 2004). This imperative has resulted from the following factors:

- The constantly changing demographics, which is changing the faces of nations. Recognizing the increasing complexity of using race and ethnicity to determine culture, the U.S. Census Bureau and the Department of Education altered their surveys to allow individuals to check multiple categories, in order to indicate their true cultural identity (Perlman & Waters, 2002).
- Differences in political structures and access to power and resources by the various groups in a society determine identity in the local context and continue to play a significant role globally regardless of whether political structures are democratic or not (Brown, 2006).
- A healthy and democratic society is a productive one (Gutman & Thompson, 2004; Layer, 2005).

However, in the U.S. one of the major challenges of democracy is the association of inequality with differences among groups and core values are generally associated with individual rights. The uneasy relationship between individual and group identity and lack of a process for a collective response to inequality directed towards a group of people indeed leads to the reaction often observed against affirmative action (Austin & Austin, 2000; Sumida and Gurin, 2001). There is a sharp contrast in other parts of the world where there are constitutions which provide special considerations to groups which have historically been excluded (Gupta, 2006).

- On-going tensions between nation-states and indigenous people's rights need to be addressed in higher education. The issues raised are not just political, but they are also about cultural survival, considering the fact that native identities predate the formation of nation-state. For example, survival of a language, religion, education, values, and identity (Champagne, 2003; Smith, 2009).

Higher education institutions in the U.S. should develop a holistic and systematic way to address historical discrimination and legacies of injustice (Short, 2003; Barkan, 2005). Institutions of higher education should use the global perspective of multicultural education as a lens to view transformation if we expect to promote institutional effectiveness. Using the global perspective as a lens, the following are strategies suggested for implementing continuous improvement if

higher education is to prepare global leaders:
- Educators at higher education institutions should identify the critical learning outcomes and competencies which graduates must have in order to be able to meet the challenges in the 21st century workplace.
- They must utilize appropriate assessment methods to determine if students are acquiring 21st century outcomes through curricular and extracurricular activities.
- Critical elements of the global perspective of multicultural education must be included in the general education core and disciplinary area curricula.
- Instructional tools and methods which promote an understanding of democracy and human rights must be incorporated in all aspects of higher learning.
- Textbooks used in college and university classrooms should openly address issues related to slavery, segregation and other injustices and provide information on ways to prevent them.
- Classroom instruction must address multicultural and diversity issues in all disciplines if college graduates are to become tomorrow's leaders.
- The learning environments must be conducive to intercultural and global interactions among a diverse student body and faculty.
- Higher education administrators and staff working with college and university students should be from different academic disciplines and

cultural backgrounds in order to expose students to various intellectual and cultural perspectives.
- Inclusive work and learning environments should be encouraged to build institutional capacity on campuses (Smith, 2009).

The application of the global perspective of multicultural education would facilitate the creation of an inclusive environment, which the Partnership for 21st century skills refers to in the *Framework* as "the 21st century learning environments". This is the kind of environment necessary for transforming higher education. Diverse perspectives and cultural dimensions cultivate respect among individuals in the campus community and benefit the institution of higher education at the organizational as well as individual levels.

They promote intellectual diversity and capital, which in turn promote institutional efficiency and effectiveness. They lead to excellence in educational quality and leadership in any setting (Combs, 2002; Iwata, 2004; Slaughter, 2004). The above strategies would facilitate the transformation of colleges and universities as they yield to the demands of the 21st century learning environments and workplace.

The Changing Role of Higher Education

Changes in the 21st century require educators and institutions of higher education to assume new roles. With the identification of the gaps in graduates knowledge and skills, educators must fully understand the key concepts and principles of multicultural education or how to incorporate them into curricular and extracurricular programs. Because of the increasing diversity of students, faculty and staff on college and university campuses today, multicultural education is more important now than ever (Ameny-Dixon, 2004). Educators and institutions of higher education today must be cognizant of the following:

- They must have a thorough understanding the various elements of the global perspective of multicultural education in order to facilitate the new roles.
- They must provide curricula which support both national and global citizenship id they are to produce graduates who are able to become global leaders.
- They must provide extracurricular activities which expose students to diverse cultures in order to reinforce and support multicultural education, global citizenship and international awareness.
- They must serve as role models in a "global learning community", in order to lead and spearhead the education of global leaders.
- They must promote educational excellence in order to positively impact the quality of the American educational system, rather than serving only as the revenue generating enterprises that they have become today.
- They must behave responsibly, as expected of model citizens in their own right; and as responsible

- organizations which consider the impact of their daily operations on the environment and planet.
- They must expand their roles from serving as isolated institutions of higher education to collaborating with other types of institutions in the nation in order to serve the needs of all students to prepare graduates who are leaders in the 21st century.
- Rather than assuming service learning and civic engagement roles as isolated colleges and universities, they should also collaborate with educational agencies in their local communities to form a "*communiversity*" in order to prepare graduates who are leaders in the 21st century.
- Rather than assuming service learning and civic engagement roles as isolated colleges and universities, they should also collaborate with colleges and universities abroad to assume the role of a "*pluriversity*" in order to prepare graduates who are leaders in the 21st century.

Educators at institutions of higher education recognize that today's graduates are faced with more global problems than their predecessors. They also recognize that graduates must have a fundamental understanding of democracy within our own nation before they can embrace democracy at the global level. They need to properly articulate the importance of culture in promoting a democracy before they can successfully participate in globalization and internationalization.

As colleges and universities work together to provide higher education opportunities to students and to serve as centers of educational excellence, utilizing the global perspectives of multicultural education will facilitate their efforts towards preparing global leaders (Ameny-Dixon, 2004). Using the global perspective of multicultural education a college and university can serve as a "*communiversity*", by becoming part of an alliance of colleges and universities where students within a region of the country are offered select associates, bachelor's and master's level programs on one campus. Each "*communiversity*" works in collaboration with others to allow students to explore high demand educational programs through specific educational pathways that prepare students for the global workplace. An example of a "*communiversity*" is the *Arizona Communiversity* which consists of Northern Arizona University, Rio Salado College, Phoenix College, Glendale Community College and West MEC.

Similarly, using the global perspective of multicultural education an institution of higher education in the U.S. can work with other colleges or universities abroad to serve as a *pluriversity* as it serves domestic as well as international students. Each *pluriversity* becomes an educational center of excellence where students interact in culturally diverse and intellectually stimulating learning environments to develop into global leaders (Rhoads & Szelenyi, 2011). An example of a *pluriversity* is the University of California, Los Angeles (UCLA), where interdisciplinary global programs are offered to both undergraduate and graduate students under the specific themes of culture and society, governance and conflict, and markets. UCLA also works with universities abroad to implement the goals of the "*pluriversity*".

Graduates Must Have 21st Century Skills to Remain Competitive

Colleges and universities recognize the importance of preparing graduates who know their role in the global workplace. For the same reasons, colleges and universities must revisit the strategies they use to prepare graduates with 21st century skills. The lack of standardization in the U.S. educational system makes it hard for colleges and universities in the U.S. to admit only college-ready students. Students are entering college with varying skill levels as they leave high schools or as adult learners returning to college. Colleges and universities should utilize the "*Framework for 21st Century Learning*" developed by the Partnership for 21st Century Skills (2009a) to reconceptualize and reinvigorate the 21st century education system. Colleges and universities should develop a holistic and systematic way to achieve 21st century student learning outcomes. Educational support services developed should allow educators to facilitate the attainment of the learning outcomes outlined in the *Framework's* major elements and components below.

- *21st Century Themes*
    - Global Awareness
    - Financial, Economic, Business and Entrepreneurial Literacy

- Civic Literacy
- Health Literacy
- Environmental Literacy

- *Learning and Innovation Skills*
  - Creativity and Innovation
  - Critical Thinking and Problem Solving
  - Communication and Collaboration

- *Core Subjects and 21st Century Themes*
  - English, Reading and Language Arts
  - World Languages
  - The Arts
  - Mathematics
  - Sciences
  - Geography
  - History
  - Government and Civics

- *Information, Media and Technology Skills*
  - Information Literacy
  - Media Literacy
  - Information and Communication Technology Literacy

- *21st Century Education Support Systems*
  - 21st Century Standards and Assessments
  - 21st Century Curriculum and Instruction
  - 21st Century Professional Development
  - 21st Century Learning Environments

- *Life and Career Skills*
  - Flexibility and Adaptability
  - Initiatives and Self-direction
  - Social and Cross-cultural Skills
  - Productivity and Accountability
  - Leadership and Responsibility

While serving as a "*communiversity*" or "*pluriversity*", a university should utilize the "*Framework for 21st century Learning*" (Partnerships for 21st Century Skills, 2009a) to promote the acquisition of 21st century skills by students. It should also utilize the *Framework* as a guideline to improve learning as it prepares graduates to develop into competitive global leaders (Partnerships for 21st Century Skills, 2009b). Incorporation of the global perspectives of multicultural education with the 21st century skills into the general education core and discipline curricula would facilitate preparation of global leaders.

CHAPTER 2

WHY THE GLOBAL PERSPECTIVE OF MULTICULTURAL EDUCATION IN HIGHER EDUCATION?

One might ask why do we need to consider the global perspective of multicultural education in the U.S. higher education system now? Or why do we need a new model for higher education in the 21st century? The answers to these questions require an understanding the U.S. educational system and the changes that are taking place in the 21st century. The answer also requires a consideration of the skills that U.S. college graduates have as they enter the global workplace. Perhaps the question we should be asking is: Are our graduates ready to be leaders in the 21st century global workplace?

Irreversible Change Has Occurred in the 21st Century Economy

The changes which have occurred in the U.S. and global economy in recent years, including the high unemployment rate presents many challenges for our graduates. These changes have prompted college and university administrators, educators and other higher education professionals to consider changes that will require bold moves in order to effect change.

- Colleges and universities are beginning to realize that they need to rethink their missions and goals if they are to prepare graduates who will become global leaders. Strategies in place are not adequate for addressing global issues.
- Colleges and universities are beginning to appreciate the benefits of diversity and respect for interaction with people from different cultural backgrounds or from different parts of the world.
- Colleges and universities are realizing that the world is changing so rapidly. Using Malcolm Gladwell's (2000) terminology, Bellanca & Bradt (2010) described the change as a "tipping point" resulting from a critical mass of circumstances coming together to set us on a new and unstoppable course". The global economy provides first hand evidence of this unstoppable change Technology, while complementing higher-level skilled workers, has replaced service workers who perform routine jobs, hence leading to the

Empowerment of more productive and creative workers (Autor, Levy, & Murnane, 2003).
- While U.S. college and university graduates do not easily adapt to the changing world, advanced economies, innovative industries and firms and high-growth jobs increasingly reward people who can adapt to organizations, products, and processes with communication, problem-solving, critical thinking skills and other 21st century skills which allow graduates to respond to organizational expectations (Partnership for 21st Century Skills, 2008).
- The U.S. remains the most competitive nation on the planet, yet it has no clear sense of direction in its educational system for securing future economic competitiveness (Scott, 2009; International Institute for Management Development, 2009).
- The warning which Science, Technology, Engineering, and Mathematics (STEM) experts in industry and higher education have echoed for decades, that the U.S. is losing ground when it comes to preparing an adequate supply of workers for critical fields has become a reality (Bellanca & Bradt, 2010). For example, today, U.S. scientists and astronauts must work with scientists and astronauts from other countries who are at the International Space Station in order to keep up in STEM and space exploration research.
- Substantial economic growth fueled by information technology in late 1980s and early 1990s seemed to have maxed out without investment in intangible

workforce assets such as new ideas, knowledge, and talent by U.S. graduates (van Ark et al., 2009).

Global Competition and Job Outsourcing

Countries which used to be superpowers but continued to disregard global change are no longer superpowers. Nations like China and Germany now lead the world's economy because they are more open to multicultural education, internationalization and globalization. Those which are still hesitant about the global perspectives of multicultural education or respect for diversity are being left academically and economically because their graduates are not being prepared to be competitive in the global workplace. U.S. college and university graduates must have 21st century skills in order to stay competitive in the global economy (van Ark et al., 2009). Graduates must be exposed to the global issues through the perspectives of multicultural education to introduce them to global competitiveness. Job outsourcing has become a national concern. Competition has become a global phenomenon; yet our graduate lack the skills needed to stay globally competitive. In an article *"American Job Outsourcing: Making other countries a lot stronger,"* Jamie Sanderson (2011) explained why American outsourcing is killing America while helping countries like Germany and China become stronger. Sharon Otterman (2004) in a Council on Foreign Relations publication *"Trade: Outsourcing Jobs"* described reasons why job outsourcing to lower-wage countries has become common practice among U.S. businesses that are seeking to cut operation costs. The short term negative impact of job outsourcing on the economy has been devastating as thousands of U.S. workers are laid-off or dislocated. Some economists argue that outsourcing will strengthen the economy in the long run, but we all know that American workers are hurt in the short run. The anxiety job outsourcing has caused among U.S. graduates and those in the workforce, particularly those who feel vulnerable to competition from well-educated workers abroad is profound considering the fact that well-educated foreign workers are willing to work for one-tenth of the wages American workers are willing to accept (Otterman, 2004). Also, to save money, U.S. companies are spending money to sponsor skilled workers from other nations to travel to the U.S. and fill positions that could be filled by America graduates. They are also taking jobs to other countries which have cheaper raw materials and lower taxes to make their products.

The availability of raw materials, technologically skilled employees, and cheaper costs of services attract these U.S. companies to operate their businesses in countries overseas. These operations benefit the countries overseas and their graduates rather than U.S. graduates. Even though economists believe that the U.S. economy will be strengthened in the long-run, job outsourcing deprives American citizens of their livelihood in the short run and the numbers are staggering. Increasing advances in technology and low-cost telecommunication tools in China, India or the Philippines means these jobs can now be completed anywhere in the world, saving the parent U.S. company 30-70% in costs. Jobs for computer programmers, data entry specialists, or help-desk operator answering calls can now be completed easily from those countries. The statistics are staggering:

- In 2008 and 2009 alone, U.S. and European companies lost nearly 1.1 million jobs in financial services, IT, HR and other white collar professions because of outsourcing which in-part resulted in the sagging economy (The Hackett Group, 2009).
- In 2009, the AMR Research Inc. reported that 80% of IT companies and enterprises planned to increase the amount of IT outsourcing and keep it the same in the coming years
- The Software Quality Experts (2010) predicted that more than 1.3 million additional jobs will be lost due to accelerated movement of work to India and other offshore locations

Global Citizenship

Regardless of the reasons for job outsourcing, it is affecting the nation's economy. The most effective way to reduce job losses is to prepare graduates with the skills similar to those possessed by graduates in the countries where the jobs are being outsourced. Exposing U.S. students to the global perspective of multicultural education would allow graduates to become global citizens.

Global citizenship has become a terminology used to describe the qualities and characteristics of individuals who are aware of the importance of living in a global community. Colleges and universities must introduce students to multicultural and global education (Cortes, 1998). The global perspective of multicultural education allows students to make connections between multicultural and global education (Merryfield, 1996). This will improve the employability of U.S. graduates in today's global economy. Higher education professionals should stand up in unity against the bigotry of those who oppose multicultural education for "selfish, racist and classist and materialistic reasons", who refer to multicultural education as a "war against western civilization", or call it a "diversity myth" simply because they oppose democracy in the American educational system. Baseless negative ideologies like those promoted by Sack and Thiel (1995) against multicultural education and diversity have kept the American higher education system and its graduates behind. Today, most educators acknowledge that multicultural education promotes pluralism, respect for all persons on the campus.

A consequence of these ideologies students in countries once referred to as "third world", such as South Korea, Finland and China, now perform better than U.S. students on the same knowledge and skills, particularly in math, science and reading literacy (TIMSS & PILRS, 2011). American graduates will be able to outcompete graduates from these countries when U.S. institutions of higher education transform their curricula and institutional practices by incorporating the global perspective of multicultural education and using it as a lens to transform the general education and disciplinary area curricula. This will allow U.S. graduates to develop the knowledge, dispositions, intercultural competencies needed for global leadership.

Multicultural Principles to Teaching and Learning

Banks et al., (2005) identified the following multicultural education principles which must be incorporated in teaching and learning of all students, to promote respect among people from different parts of the world.

- Students should learn about complex relationships between unity and diversity in their local communities, the nation, and the world the world
- Students should learn about the ways in which people in their community, nation, and region are increasingly interdependent with other people around the world and are connected to the economic, political, cultural, environmental, and technological changes taking place across the planet.
- The teaching of human rights should underpin citizenship education courses and programs in multicultural nation-states.
- Students should be taught knowledge about democracy and democratic institutions and provide opportunities to practice democracy.

Multicultural Education and Internationalization

For students to make the transition from understanding domestic democracy to understanding global democracy and to internationalization, students must understand the global perspective of multicultural education. Olsen et al. (2007) described common goals and learning outcomes for both multicultural education and internationalization, including the shared nature of the work involved and the shared learning outcomes. She found that embracing the global perspectives of multicultural education lead to the attainment of the following global learning outcomes:

- Global knowledge
- Global perspective consciousness and intercultural sensitivity
- Global intercultural communication skills

The key concepts and principles of the global perspectives of multicultural education are associated with the global learning outcomes which global leaders possess. Institutions of higher education need to incorporate these concepts in diverse disciplinary areas and use them as lenses in the college and university curriculum, including history, literature, economics, religion, geography, and the science, technology, engineering, and mathematics (STEM) disciplines to incorporate the key concepts of and principles of global education.

Shaw et al. (2009) found that faculty in the English, history, sociology, anthropology; ethnic studies and women's studies had a natural affinity for diversity. In contrast, faculty in the science, technology, engineering, and mathematics (STEM) and professional disciplines perceived their work as limited to technical skills and a certain canon of disciplinary knowledge. When her team continued to conduct curriculum transformation workshops around the country, examples of how faculty, particularly those in STEM disciplines can incorporate the global perspectives of multicultural education into STEM education stimulated great discussions.

Institutions of higher education need to be in compliance with diversity requirements as provided in the HEA (1965) and as required by the U.S. Department of Education and accrediting agencies in order to meet accreditation requirements. Multicultural education provides an avenue to promote respect among students, faculty and staff in the campus community. Using the global perspective of multicultural education can enhance an institution's efforts to meet federal and accreditation requirements related to diversity.

As will be discussed in the next chapter, transformation of higher education is necessary if U.S. higher education institutions plan to prepare graduates who are global leaders. This transformation must include restructuring as well as overcoming some of the challenges embedded in the key features of U.S. institutions of higher education as presented in the next chapter.

CHAPTER 3

KEY FEATURES OF AMERICAN INSTITUTIONS OF HIGHER EDUCATION

There are many variations in the sizes, types, missions, and curricula of individual institutions of higher education in the U.S. However, there are four key features which differentiate American institutions of higher education from those in other countries. The following are the key features which differentiate American institutions of higher education from those in other countries of the world.

- The U.S. higher education system is an extremely large and diverse enterprise compared to higher education systems in other countries. For example, in the 2005-2006 academic year only, there were 6,814 accredited postsecondary institutions, which enrolled over 20 million students.

Approximately 3,400 of these institutions were traditional public universities and colleges and the remaining 3,414 were private career colleges (ACE, 2007). These institutions have produced a U.S. graduate population of about 36 percent with associate degrees and approximately 25 percent with undergraduate degrees (U.S. Department of Education, 2006).

- There is no national system of higher education. The federal government has a very limited role in higher education. Each of the 50 states has their own systems of control over public institutions but very limited control over the private institutions operated in each state. Although some state governments grant licenses to higher education institutions, academic legitimacy is controlled mainly by the regional accreditation agencies and voluntary accountability processes controlled by non-profit organizations.
- The marketplace is the key external driver of institutional policies and behaviors. There are no uniform policies or expectations. Every institution of higher education in the U.S. establishes its niche by creating its own unique mission or priorities depending on the needs of the students it serves, its type, sources of funding, and geographical location.
- Degree completion at the undergraduate level (and to a large extent at the graduate level) is determined

by a system of courses and credits. Students enroll in individual courses every semester (or quarter) each of which is assigned a certain amount of credit, determined by the number of class hours the course meets each week (most often 50-minute "hours" or its equivalent) as determined by the Carnegie System of credits.

Types of Higher Education Institutions in the U.S.

According to the American Council on Education (ACE), there are four major types of institutions of higher education in the U.S.

- Two-year colleges are usually community or professional colleges which grant associate degrees to students upon their completion of a minimum of 60 credit hours of coursework (or its equivalent).
- Four-year undergraduate institutions are bachelor degree-granting institutions. Some four-year colleges may also have specialized degree programs and graduate programs.
- Graduate degree-granting institutions are usually referred to as Universities because they provide research programs which lead to the Masters and Doctor of Philosophy degrees. The type of degree depends on the disciplinary area and the amount of research involved in the attainment of the
graduate degree.

- Other types of higher education institutions include military academies, specialized institutions (such as Medical Colleges, Engineering Colleges, and Seminaries and Theological Colleges), and Land-grant public universities, Historically Black Colleges and Universities and Tribal Colleges.

In addition to the above typical domestic campuses, most American Universities today have sister campuses abroad where American students can travel and immerse themselves in international cultures and learn together. To improve their effectiveness in promoting global education, these sister satellite campuses need to be transformed by incorporating the global perspectives of multicultural education into their curricular and extracurricular learning activities.

Governance and Public Policy Issues in Higher Education

The U.S. does not have a central Ministry of Education which controls the various Colleges and Universities. Some of the institutions are autonomous, self-governing organizations while others are affiliated with federal, government agencies. Every institution of higher education has a President or Chancellor as the administrative helm who answers to a Board of Trustees. However, control, governance and policy issues in higher education in the U.S. relate to the following:

- *"Accountability"* – Every institution of higher education is expected by the federal government, state legislators, policy makers and the public to be accountable for student learning and transparency in daily operations. Given the rising costs of higher education, funders, students and parents also expect colleges and universities to be responsible for student learning, graduation rates, the balance between teaching and research and commitment to improving the communities in which they are located, thus the concept of a *"communiversity"*. For the latter reason, most colleges and universities encourage current students as well as graduates to be engaged in service learning or civic activities within the university community.
- *"Access and Equity"* – Like in other countries, in the US, there is widespread public belief in the power of education in facilitating social and economic change. For example, data provides evidence that young people from low-income backgrounds who complete a bachelor's degree earn similar income and employment as those from affluent backgrounds. However, with high rate of unemployment in every state in the nation today, transformation is needed to ensure that graduates gain expanded skills to be gainfully employed locally or globally.
- *"Affordability"* – Is an area of focus in today's economy and has also been a long-standing priority in higher education. Federal financial aid allows students to be able to afford higher education.

However, some federal officials and state legislators are requiring more accountability from colleges and universities whose students receive federal aid (ACE, 2004, Haycock, 2006).

- *"Lifelong learning"* – In a global marketplace driven by technology and innovation, every graduate is expected to be a life-long learner. This concept has become an important public policy issues because it is a key to success in the local and global workplace. This issue is even more critical among adult learners, and is closely related to affordability, access and equity. It is believed that lifelong learning is critical for the economic well-being of a nation.
- *"Internationalization"* – The growth of technological resources, telecommunications, increased economic interdependence between nations and globalization is forcing colleges and universities to rethink their current curriculum, research and service functions. The changes colleges and universities are experiencing in the 21st century will require transformation in all three areas in order to be able produce global leaders.

Policy issues related to accountability and compliance as required by the U.S. Department of Education are handled by the accreditation agencies, which in turn report to the U.S. Department of Education. Through independent processes, every institution of higher education also submits institutional data to its regional accreditation agency and to the Department of Education's

Integrated Postsecondary Education System (IPEDS) which is managed by the Institute of Education Sciences.

Public institutions of higher education can also post information about undergraduate student experiences at their institutions, on the Voluntary System of Accountability system (VSA) template called the College Portrait, in order to provide the public, parents and students with information about these public institutions. Similarly, private institutions of higher education can post information about their institutions on the University and College Accountability Network (U-CAN) in order to inform the public, parents and students with information about their institutions.

Externally, academic quality at each institution is affirmed by regional accreditation agencies, which establish academic standards and confer on each institution acknowledgement of academic excellence. Internally, academic integrity is overseen collectively by the faculty, Deans, and the Provost or V.P. for Academic Affairs. Institutions with professional academic programs also seek specialized accreditation by the appropriate accreditation agencies. The regional and specialized accreditation agencies answer to the U.S. Department of Education.

The U.S. Department of Education with recommendation from the National Advisory Committee on Institutional Quality and Integrity (NACIQI), works with accreditation agencies to enforce policies provided in the Higher Education Opportunity Act of 1965, also referred to as the Higher Education Act of 1965 (HEA, 1965). The HEA (1965), which was signed into United States Law on November 8, 1965 and has been reauthorized several times, provides colleges and universities guidelines on appropriate policy and practices. The HEA (1965) was intended:

> "to strengthen the educational resources of our colleges and universities and to provide financial assistance for students in post-secondary and higher education".

Through the HEA (1965), federal funding was increased to colleges and universities, scholarships and low-interest loans, and a National Teachers Corps were created. The National Advisory Committee on Institutional Quality and Integrity (NACIQI) advises the U.S. secretary of Education on matters related to higher education accreditation and the eligibility and certification process for higher education institutions to participate in the federal student aid programs.

Higher education policy issues are also supervised by non-profit higher education organizations, which work with the Department of Education while serving as voices for the accrediting agencies for the various types of higher education institutions. These non-profit organizations also work directly with colleges and universities to guide them on accountability and compliance issues. Examples of such organizations include the following:

- The Council *for Higher Education Accreditation (CHEA),* provides national advocacy for self- regulation of academic quality through accreditation.

The CHEA certifies the quality of higher education accrediting organizations, including regional, faith-based, private career and programmatic accrediting organizations.
- The *American Council on Education (ACE)*, is the major coordinating body for all U.S. higher education institutions regardless of their type, and provides leadership influences public policy through advocacy, research, and program initiatives on key higher education issues.
- The *National Association of Independent Colleges and Universities (NAICU)*, serves as a unified voice of independent higher education and represent private colleges and universities on policy issues affecting student aid, taxation, and government regulation.
- The *Commission on Independent Colleges and Universities (CICU)* is a statewide association representing the public policy interests of the chief executives of more than 100 independent colleges and universities in New York State.

The reader should note that the above list of organizations also reflects the diversity in the types of higher education institutions. Because of the wide variation in the types of colleges and universities and lack of uniformity in the educational programs offered, regional and specialized accreditation agencies must certify institutions and professional program degree offerings. A detailed account of accreditation requirements related to diversity and how the global perspectives of multicultural education can be utilized to help colleges and universities in meeting these accreditation requirements are discussed later. The next chapter will discuss how multicultural education promotes global education and why they matter today more than ever.

CHAPTER 4

GLOBAL INTERACTIONS MATTER TODAY MORE THAN EVER

Population changes at the state, national, and regional levels in the United States are forcing educators, policy makers and politicians to rethink our current perceptions of citizenship, leadership and our place and responsibility to planet earth. We increasingly find ourselves living in communities similar to a "global village". Technological advances have increased the pace at which the "world is getting smaller" in the social context. The rapidly increasing interconnections among all nations in the world today, as we face common global concerns related to the ecosystem, nuclear weapons, terrorism, human rights, and scarce national resources demands a global approach to finding solutions to these global issues (Rhoads & Szelenyi, 2011).

In a social context, everyone has heard of the saying that "the world is getting smaller". What does this mean for any of us living today or for the nations of the world today? Can anyone alive today function in isolation? Is it possible to ignore what is going on in the neighboring states? Is it possible to ignore the economy or changes related to our educational system, technological and scientific advances taking place around us or in other parts of the world?

Today, people can travel from one end of the world to another within days. They can use the Internet with other social media such as Facebook, MySpace, Twitter, or using the telephone in the form of cell phones or landlines, Skype have made it easier for people from different parts of the world to communicate with each other within seconds (Quicksey, 2009). Technology has brought societies from different parts of the world closer together as people now share cultures, ideas, and beliefs more easily with each other than ever before. Compared to the 1960's and 1970's when the avenue to free speech and other forms of social justice depended on sharing information through sit-ins, freedom rides, and freedom marches or boycotts, today's social platforms allow information to spread quickly across the globe in the shortest time possible. The power of these social platforms cannot be underestimated. For example, they played major roles in recent Middle-Eastern political riots which led to the overthrow of the governments of Egypt, Libya, Tunisia, and Algeria and continues to play major roles in countries like Syria and Iran. In recent months and weeks, students and opposition leaders in Iran have used

Facebook and *Twitter* to spread their message and share images about their political demands. Places that once seemed remote and people whose cultures once seemed unreachable are now only "a click away" and virtually next door as a result of advances in technology.

The Impact of Technology on Global Interactions

The impact of technology was evident at the time of writing this book, as protests erupted in almost every city in the U.S. These protests spread rapidly from the east coast in the form of "Occupy Wall Street" in New York to the west coast in the form of "Occupy Los Angeles". They also spread from the U.S. to European cities where the protests became "Occupy London", "Occupy Paris", Occupy Berlin", etc... and to regions of the world including the African Continent becoming "Occupy Cairo" and down to Australia as "Occupy Sydney" etc. The movement spread like fire to various parts of the world. With the aid of technology providing instant information to everyone all over the world, the whole world seemed "to be on fire". The world seems much smaller, flatter, and more connected than ever because people were able to use various forms of social media and technological tools such as videos, photos, podcasts, chat rooms, message boards, widgets, and blogs to share information. At institutions of Higher Education today, students have more technological tools available to them to promote social change than any of their predecessors. Through the Internet College and University students are able to share their messages locally and abroad. Working independently on their campuses students can now broadcast videos, photos, and headline news about anything that is happening on their campuses including exchange of discipline-specific information about what they are studying. Figure 1 below provides the various social media platforms which are used by students, teachers, researchers and other professionals in various fields all over the world today.

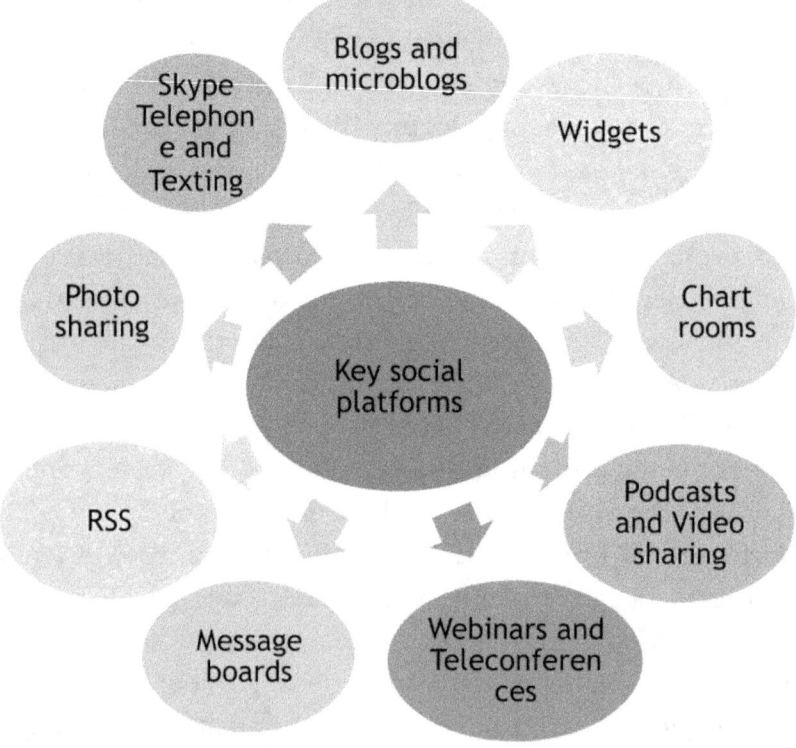

Figure 1: Key social platforms resulting from advanced technology in the 21st Century (Adopted from Angel Quicksey, 2009)

The educational impact and advantages of global interactions using the various social platforms are enormous. The short term advantages of global communications and interactions are that students and instructors at Colleges and Universities at one part of the world can exchange information with students and instructors from another part of the world. Similarly, through webinars and teleconferences, researchers from different parts of the world can share results of their research. This kind of exchange gives students the ability to grasp and distinguish the difference between their own culture and knowledge and the culture and knowledge of the students from another culture, and enables each group to positively impact and improve their of their knowledge and skills using the lessons learned from students from other cultures.

The Impact of Global Communication

Jerome Bruner (2006) described the advantages of such global communication as enormous. In the long run, global interactions have the following advantages.

- It accelerates self-awareness and intercultural awareness hence promotes intercultural competencies.
- It promotes global partnerships through professional exchanges.
- It accelerates global communication skills or the ability to provide and access information across cultures through speaking, listening, and reading
and writing. These skills are vital and critical in

the business environment where language and cultural barriers impact efficiency.
- It increases productivity for the industries involved because of the intellectual diversity in mental and physical resources used to solve problems.
- It brings together professionals from across the world to share best practices, research, and technologies to create a better world for human kind.
- It allows educators and policy makers from across the globe to work together in developing projects, programs and possibilities in addressing global issues.

The economic impact of the global interactions depends on the issues being addressed. However, there are more advantages to global interactions than there are disadvantages. Jeff Rubin (2009) predicted the impact of oil supply and demand on globalization, Dagmar Lorenz (2011) described how a revolution in communications has produced the global village. Using media such *Facebook*, *Twitter* and *MySpace* allows people from different parts of the world to communicate with each other. *Info villages.com* has become the platform for professionals such Engineers, businessmen and like-minded people who are traveling for humanitarian or non-humanitarian reasons to communicate freely with those back home to inform colleagues of every turn and twist in their travel. As the world becomes smaller, technology becomes very important in promoting global communication. In the next chapter, examples of how we live in a global community are provided.

CHAPTER 5

WE LIVE IN GLOBAL COMMUNITIES TODAY

The recent rhetoric about global citizenship, the spreading global economic crises sweeping across the world and never seems to go away and with more resources being devoted by world nations today to combat terrorism, nations need to work together more than ever before. The world has become interconnected now than ever before. Disastrous natural events such as earthquakes, tsunamis, and tornadoes no longer affect only one part of the world, their impact are now felt in all other parts of the world when economic resources are cut off. These conditions make it very difficult for world leaders to ignore global issues.

With every passing day, we seem to be living in a world that is increasingly becoming smaller and smaller. Predictions that were made in the early 1990's about living in a "global village" seems to have become a reality everyday today. Educational systems especially those in the United States, will need to keep up with the changes going on in society today in order to be able to prepare graduates who have the skills to lead in the 21st century.

Composition of Global Communities

Most educators know about the 20th century publication *Who Lives in the "Global Village"* by Donella Meadows (1997), in which he provided estimates to reflect the number of people from different nationalities, with different languages and religious affiliations that would be found in a global village composed of one thousand people from different regions of the world. Meadows (1997) introduced us to the concept of the global village, when he described a global village as an increasingly diverse society with people from various nationalities composed of different racial and ethnic backgrounds, speaking different languages and practicing different types of world religions. He described the nationality of origin in a global village with one thousand (1,000) people as composed of 584 (58%) Asians, 124 (12%) Africans, 95 (10%) East and West Europeans, 84 (8%) Latin Americans, 55 (5.5%) Soviets including Lithuanians, Latvians, Estonians and other Soviets, 52 (5.2%) North American including Americans and Canadians, 6 (0.6%) Australians and New Zealanders. A pie chart representing the composition of a global village with 1, 000 people based on their nationality is shown in Figure 2 on the following page.

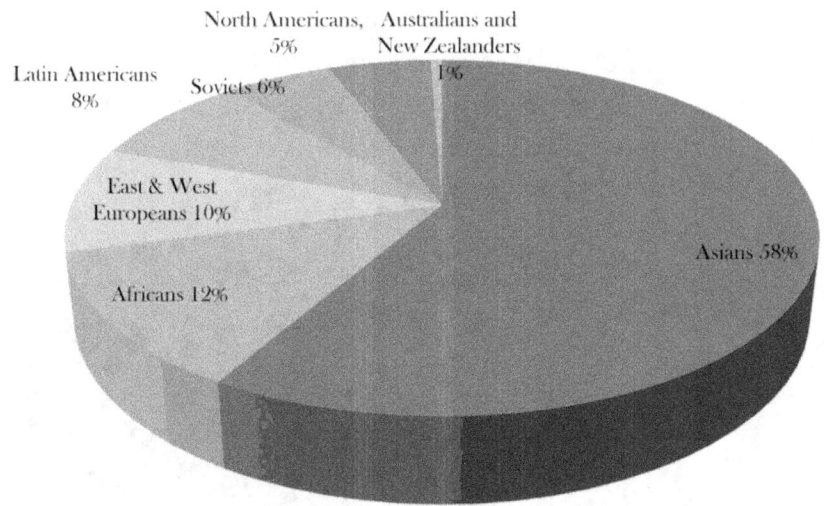

Figure 2: Nationalities of 1,000 people living in a Global Village

As represented in the pie chart above and much to our surprise, there would be more Asians in a global village with one thousand people than North Americans. This is contrary to our way of thinking, because we always think that there are more North Americans or people of Western European origin than every other nationality is a minority. Based on the major world languages spoken by people in different parts of the world, Meadows (1997) predicted that in a "global village" with one thousand (1,000) people there would be 165 (17%) people who would speak Mandarin, 86 (.9%) people who speak English, 83 (.8%) would speak Hindu, 64 (0.6%) would who speak Spanish, 58 (.5%) would speak Russian, 37 people who speak Arabic, and the remaining combined number of 507 (51%) would be people who speak the common languages of Bengali, Portuguese, Indonesian, Japanese, German, French and 200 other world languages. The pie chart in Figure 3 below represents the languages spoken by the various people in the world.

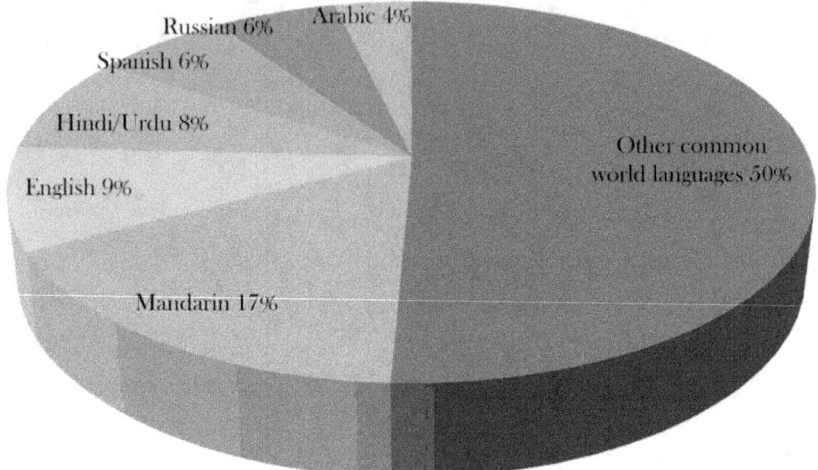

Figure 3: Languages of 1,000 people living in a Global Village

Based on major world religions, if you were to consider a global village with one thousand (1,000) people there would be 329 (33%) Christians (including 187 Catholics, 84 Protestants and 31 Orthodox). There would be 178 (18%) Muslims, 167 (17%) "Non-religious" people, 132 (13%) Hindus, 60 (6%) Buddhists, 45 (4%) Atheists, 3 (0.3%) Jews, and 86 (9%) would belong to all other small world religions. The reader should note that contrary to the general belief that there are more Christians in the world than non-Christians, demographic statistics actually show that there are more non-Christians (67%) in the world than Christians (33%). These religious demographics are represented in Figure 4.

Ch. 5: We Live in Global Communities Today

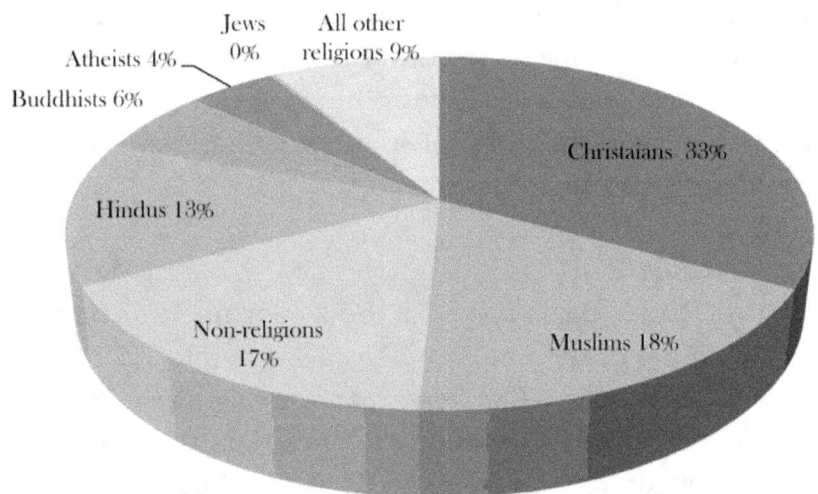

Figure 4: Religions of 1,000 people living in a Global Village

We should not be surprised to find that today, it is easier to live in a global community because of technological advances which are allowing people from different regions of the world. Also today, it is easier to learn about other cultures, languages, religions than ever before. Knowledge of the global perspective of multicultural education facilitates interactions in a global community. This knowledge also facilitates global education, globalization and internationalization and allows us to communicate more easily with people from other parts of the world.

College and University Campuses Are Global Communities

Using the global village model, several institutions of higher education in the U.S. today have begun to create global learning communities on their campuses. Examples of some of the U.S. college campuses with global living-learning communities or centers in order to begin applying the principles of the global perspective of multicultural education are:

- Yulee Hall Global Living-Learning Community under the Department of Housing and Residential Education, University of Florida, Gainesville, FL., open to any student who is interested in becoming a "citizen on the world"
- Baylor University Global Community and Living-Learning Center, Wako, Texas with 177 undergraduate students
- Georgetown University's global living community with 22 undergraduate students
- Jacksonville University's Global Connections Learning Community with 26 students, 13 international students and 13 American students
- Saint Mary's College of California's Global Living Learning, located in Claeys North Hall, open to variable numbers of students each year

Goals of the Global Learning Communities

- The Baylor University Global Community Living-Learning Center, which allows students to explore other cultures in a community and as individuals. Membership in the global learning center allows students to learn about the global cultures by:
  - Living with internationally-minded friends and students from other countries
  - Getting immersed in a target language

by attending faculty-led Lingo groups which are organized specifically global community living-learning members
- Deepening their spiritual life by learning about other religions
- Developing leadership through community service
- Participating in global events such as community dinners with students and faculty from other cultures, world cinema nights, and other global village activities
- Completes a global community living-learning cohort course which enhances their understanding of the world and its dynamic cultures. Upon completion of this course, the student is able to:
  - Research analyze, and communicate any given culture in while having the awareness of how to adapt to that culture
  - Think critically and strategically about his/her role as a global citizen
  - Understand and appreciate how service impacts community and how community transforms the individual
  - Explain how personal development occurs through life-long learning

- The Yulee Hall Global Living-Learning Community under the Department of Housing and Residential Education at the University of Florida has the primary goal of developing globally competent learners who exhibit the following characteristics:

- Exhibit awareness of one's own cultural values, beliefs, attitudes, biases, and stereotypes and the impact of these on others.
- Demonstrate knowledge about world history, current events, global economics and sustainability
- Acknowledge and respect existence of different cultural values, beliefs, and attitudes
- Recognize that people are interconnected and globally interdependent
- Communicate and collaborate effectively in a cross-cultural environment
- Accept responsibility for active world citizenship

These colleges and universities and others not mentioned here have recognized the importance of global communities, and are utilizing their residential programs to allow both multicultural and global education to be implemented with to both American and international students. These activities allow students to develop important global skills and skills for cross-cultural communication and global learning as they interact with other students and faculty in the global earning communities. These colleges and universities have recognized that campus environments reflect the changes taking place in the global arena. The challenge which still remains for these colleges and universities and others that have not yet developed global living-learning programs is how to expand these global education programs so that every student on their campus has the opportunity to participate in order to be a successful graduate in the global workplace. It is, therefore imperative that the global perspective of multicultural education be utilized to facilitate campus learning if we expect our graduates to work well with graduates from other parts of the world through an understanding and use of global perspective of multicultural education, intercultural awareness and competence.

In a study conducted by Oxfam in Great Britain (2006) a global citizen was described as one who is aware of and has an understanding of the world around him/her, values diversity, is involved in the community on a variety of levels, and does not tolerate social injustice. He/she develops habits that make the world more equitable and sustainable and accepts responsibility for his/her actions. In the United States, an increasing number of Colleges and Universities are engaging in expansion of international exchange programs with countries abroad. These exchange programs would greatly enhance the global learning centers on these campuses if the motivation for such exchanges were for real global learning and human interactions and solidarity rather than the prevailing view of traveling for profit and site-seeing or tourism (Strompquist, 2002).

In a study involving focus groups of students in British Columbia, researchers found that participants described global citizenship as a "consciousness and commitment" to the principle of one planet, in which the interests of individuals are viewed in light of the overall needs of the planet" (Lyakhovetska, 2004).

The following concepts become very important in the global learning community and international exchange programs to allow students from different counties travel and learn together:

- Sense of shared purpose
- Respect for differences
- Agreement of core values
- Intercultural communication
- Shared responsibility
- Participation Acceptance
- Collaboration
- Conscious choice
- Commitment
- Reciprocity
- Openness
- Accountability
- Trust
- Efficacy

As colleges and universities implement global learning communities, a key question to ask in order to assess if goals are being met is: "To what extent are students in the global community developing the above characteristics?" In order to answer the above question, colleges and universities should help students to understand intercultural interactions using an interdisciplinary approach. Students should be encouraged to examine key forces shaping lives in today's fast-changing times by using the global perspective of multicultural education to help them acquire global knowledge.

Despite increased numbers of cultural and international exchange programs between American colleges and universities abroad, local identities are still constructed on the basis of "us-versus-them" ideology by students and higher education professionals. This is evident every time you listen to participants of these exchange programs describing events related to a nationalistic, religious or ethnic conflict or a mixture of the three in various parts of the world (Rhoades & Szelenyi, 2011). In some instances, such trips seem to reinforce stereotypes towards other cultures.

Colleges and universities should assume a central role in challenging the foundations of "us-versus-them" ideology and forging more expansive notions of citizenship. They should play a central role in preparing tomorrow's leaders and serving as the "social conscience" for societies in which they are located. In addition, Marginson (2010) argued that a more critical in today's "global connectedness" and "global flows of people, ideas, knowledge, and capital" than ever before and colleges and universities should play a role in the production, management, and application of knowledge. In the next chapter, multicultural education is defined. The conceptual framework, concepts and principles of the global perspective of multicultural education is explained and compared to those of the assimilation or "melting pot" perspective in order to explain which one is more useful for promoting global citizenship and preparing global leaders.

CHAPTER 6

WHAT IS MULTICULTURAL EDUCATION?

Multicultural education is an approach to teaching and learning that is based on democratic values that affirm cultural pluralism within culturally diverse societies in an interdependent world (Bennett, 1999). Regardless of the subject students are being taught, multicultural education is based on the assumption that the primary goal of public education is to foster intellectual, social, and personal development of all students to their fullest potential.

Several studies conducted at institutions of higher education have identified several long-term benefits of multicultural education (Ameny-Dixon, 2004; Gollnick & Chinn, 2002; Hirsh, 1987; Johnson & Johnson, 2002; Larson & Ovando, 2001; Levy, 1997; Quiseberry, McIntyre, & Duhon, 2002; Shulman & Mesa-Bains, 1993; Silverman, Welty, & Lyon, 1994), have identified long-term benefits of multicultural education as follows:

- Multicultural education increases productivity because a variety of mental resources are available for completing the same tasks. It promotes cognitive and moral growth among all the people involved.
- Multicultural education increases creative problem-solving skills through the different perspectives applied to same problems to reach solutions.
- Multicultural education increases positive relationships through achievement of common goals, respect, appreciation, and commitment to equality among the intellectuals at institutions of higher education.
- Multicultural education decreases stereotyping and prejudice through direct contact and interactions among diverse individuals.
- Multicultural education renews vitality of society through the richness of the different cultures of its members and fosters development of a broader and more sophisticated view of the world.

Defined in the sociopolitical context, multicultural education is an on-going process of comprehensive school reform and basic education for all students. It challenges and rejects racism and other forms of discrimination in schools and society. It affirms all forms of pluralism (including ethnic, linguistic, religious, economic, gender, age and ability) that students, their communities, teachers represent. Multicultural education permeates the curriculum and instructional strategies used in K-12 schools and institutions of higher education, the interactions among teachers, students, and parents, and the very way schools and institutions of higher education conceptualize the nature of teaching and learning. Using critical pedagogy as the underlying philosophy, it focuses on knowledge, reflection, and actions as the basis for social change and promotes the democratic principles of social justice.

Approaches Used to Promote to Multicultural Education

The four approaches that have been used to promote multicultural education in K-12 schools to promote curriculum reform include the contribution, additive, transformation, and action approaches. These approaches are provided below in figure 5.

From no integration of multicultural education in
the assimilation perspective of multicultural education

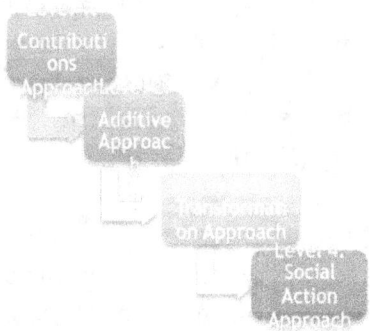

To total classroom integration of multicultural education after use of all four levels of approaches in the global perspective of multicultural education

Figure 5: Approaches to Multicultural Education (Banks, 2002)

The contribution approach reflects the least amount of integration of multicultural education. It is close to doing nothing. Textbooks and activities which show heroes and celebration of events at specific times in various cultures may be selected and used in the classroom during specific holidays, but the activities are not part of the curriculum. In the additive approach, content, concepts, themes and perspectives are added to the curriculum without changing the basic structure of the curriculum.

Literature about people from other cultures is incorporated into the mainstream curriculum without transforming mainstream thinking. For example, incorporating a Native American's perspective about Thanksgiving would be would be an additive approach. In the transformation approach students are encouraged to view concepts, themes, issues and problems from several ethnic perspectives in order to critically think about diversity as a basic premise. Lastly but not least, the social action approach combines the transformation approach with activities that promote social change. Students view social problems from different perspectives and take action to solve the problem. For example, to address issues related to poverty among a particular group of people, students design action plans such as food and clothing drives to provide the people involved with food and clothing (Banks, 1999).

If none of the approaches are used in the curriculum, lack of integration of multicultural education creates a general sense of inequality among students, particularly those from the microcultures. In the next chapter, a discussion of the assimilation or "melting-pot" perspective, which preserves the mainstream culture of the Western European or Anglo-Saxon people, is discussed.

CHAPTER 7

WHY IS MULTICULTURAL EDUCATION MORE IMPORTANT NOW THAN EVER?

Policy and recommendations related to multicultural education and diversity in higher education exists (HEA, 1965; ACE, 2008; AAAS, 2000), however, postsecondary educators have not been held accountable for multicultural education to the same extent as K-12 grade educators. Policy makers, educators and researchers involved in promoting multicultural education have found that very few colleges and university professional have training in multicultural education (Banks, 1987; Banks et al., 1993; Boise, 1993; Clark & Gorski, T., 2002; Cushner, et al., 2000; Duhon et al., 2002; Duhon-Boudreaux, 1998).

These educators and researchers also found that many higher education professionals perceive diversity requirements as a compliance issue than a commitment issue. Colleges and universities worry about being in compliance with federal or accreditation requirements for diversity only when expecting a federal audit or an accreditation visit rather than viewing diversity requirements as part of the institution's daily operations.

Multicultural education is an inclusive teaching and learning process which engages all students in developing a strong sense of self-esteem, discovering empathy for persons of diverse cultural backgrounds, and experiencing equitable opportunities to achieve their fullest potential (Tiedt & Tiedt, 199). In order to emphasize the importance of multicultural education in our educational system, Sonia Nieto (1996) described the basic characteristics of education as follows:

- Multicultural education is basic education of all students
- Multicultural education is antiracist education that must be taught to all students
- Multicultural education is important for all educators and students
- Multicultural education is pervasive and permeates throughout all sectors of the educational system
- Multicultural education is education for social justice
- Multicultural education is an ongoing process; changes adopted must reflect changes in society
- Multicultural education is critical pedagogy

While the goals of multicultural education have not changed, the process used to achieve the goals of multicultural education has changed over time, depending on the changes that are taking place in society. Until recently, multicultural education focused primarily on the equity pedagogy as a means of counteracting the problems created by the assimilation or "melting-pot" perspective of multicultural education. Today, with the rapidly increasing interconnections among all nations in the world, particularly as we face global issues related to the ecosystem, nuclear weapons, terrorism, human rights, and scarce national resources, the scope of multicultural education must be broadened to include global perspectives.

Institutions of higher education are models for the communities and nations in which they are located and can serve as the loci for embracing for the global perspectives of multicultural education. In the next chapters, the assimilation and global perspectives of multicultural education are described with the extent to which they are useful in promoting global education and for developing global citizens. Each chapter will also show how each perspective can be used to provide equal educational opportunities, motivate students, and promote academic achievement among all students. Most importantly, the reader should note that the application of the global perspective of multicultural education does not require creating quotas for any group of students, nor does it warrant admission of unqualified students or graduation of underprepared graduates (Ameny-Dixon, 2004).

Rather application of multicultural education in higher education requires making a conscious effort to reach out to students from all cultural backgrounds who meet the academic requirements for admission into a college program order to build a diverse, healthy and intellectually stimulating learning environment (Banks, 2005). The success of higher education and the strength of the U.S. democracy in the global arena will depend on how colleges and universities practice the global perspective of multicultural education. Postsecondary institutions which embrace the global perspective of multicultural education benefit from this practice by becoming models of a democratic pluralistic society, and models for schools and communities in which they are located (Ameny- Dixon, 2004).

Multicultural Education and Diversity as Accreditation Requirements

Institutions of higher education are responsible for training the teachers who go out to the schools to teach all students, though their teacher education programs, regardless of the students' socio-economic, racial and ethnic backgrounds or language, physical ability (or disability), age and cultural differences. As a result of the practices adopted during school reform, the National Committee for the Accreditation of Teacher Education (NCATE) has recognized the importance of diversity and collaborated with Departments of Education to require that all teacher preparation programs with comprehensive discussions of inter-group relations, stereotypes, biases, discriminations, and prejudices and assurance of respect for human rights. NCATE accreditation requires teacher preparation programs to prepare teacher candidates who demonstrate knowledge, skills and dispositions to help all students in a diverse society learn. NCATE standard related to diversity, specifically NCATE Unit Standard 4 states that:

> "The unit designs, implements, and evaluates curriculum and experiences for candidates to acquire and apply the knowledge, skills, and dispositions necessary to help all students learn. These experiences include working with diverse higher education and school faculty, diverse candidates, and diverse students in K-12 schools"

Recognizing the role diversity in promoting democracy and shared governance, accrediting agencies for higher education institutions now require colleges and universities to show evidence of diversity in the administrative leadership, faculty and staff as well as student body. The Higher Learning Commission of the North Central Association of Schools and Colleges states that:

> "The vitality that characterizes the higher education system in the United States is derived from the diversity found within the universe of organizations that comprise it, ... and recognizes that the diversity inherent among the people of the United States enriches American higher education and contributes to the capacity that students

develop for living in a pluralistic and interdependent world."

The HLC also requires institutions of higher education to provide evidence of diversity in various forms and areas of operation within an institution, ranging from differences in organizational mission and educational levels to differences in the ideas, viewpoints, values, religious beliefs, cultural backgrounds, race, gender, age sexual orientation, human capacity, and ethnicity of those who attend or work in the organization. The HLC believes that individual and group differences add richness to the teaching and learning and challenge them.

The Southern Association of Colleges and Schools (SACS) statement on diversity is as follows:

> "Diversity is not an abstract concept; it is a true picture of an ever-changing national demographic landscape that reflects every sector of society. Institutions of higher education mirror diversity through their missions, their structures, and their students, faculty and staff. Diversity in higher education is enriched by the distinct mission of each institution... as an asset to higher education, its benefits are numerous. Some of the outcomes of achieving and embracing diversity in higher education are as follows:

- Assists institutions in achieving their mission
- Sustains a quality learning environment and quality educational experience
- Creates an inclusive learning environment that empowers students
- Develops a work force that contributes to the social and economic competitiveness of the country
- Embraces the foundation of a democratic society

The Western Association of Colleges (WASC)'s Accrediting Commission for Senior Colleges and Universities statement on diversity is as follows:

> "The word diversity has been used frequently in discussions of higher education policy in the last 70 years...to refer to the variety of American institutions of higher education-their varying missions, pedagogies, and constituencies. It has been used to refer to the enrollment of students from various regions of the U.S. and nations of the world. It is useful to think of diversity in higher education as having three vital and related dimensions: 1) Representation; 2) the nature of the campus community; and 3) the impact of group membership on both individual and content of academic scholarship and study....representation in terms of diversity concerns representation of different groups in the various constituencies of a college or university – its

student body, faculty, staff and governing board, concerns that are closely linked to the challenge of achieving educational equity. Community on campus concerns the character of the academic community that emerges through interaction of people of different backgrounds and points of view; an effective community calls for respect and cooperation among its various groups. Group membership concerns the extent to which group differences and affiliations should be recognized and affirmed by colleges and Universities"

In summary, multicultural education benefits all members of the campus community. It creates an environment of respect among the various groups, promotes respect for diversity, promotes intercultural communications and equips faculty with approaches that allow that to implement curriculum reform in order to sustain academic quality without compromising the content taught. In summary, the benefits multicultural education in promoting diversity outweighs the myths of shared culture created by the assimilation perspective when various groups are denied participation in the development of a shared culture. These benefits are reinforced by the following recommendations by the higher education accrediting agencies:

- Diversity enriches educational experience by allowing students to learn from those whose

experiences, beliefs, and perspectives are different from their own.
- Diversity promotes personal growth in a healthy society by challenging stereotypical preconceptions. It encourages critical thinking, and helps students to communicate effectively with people from different cultures.
- Diversity strengthens the campus community and workplace. It prepares students to become good citizens within an increasingly complex global society and fosters mutual respect, team work, builds communities whose members are judged by the quality of their character and contributions.
- Diversity enhances America's competitiveness in the global marketplace.

Accountability for Multicultural Education in Higher Education

Until recently, colleges and universities did not see multicultural education as an important area of focus in academic programs. For these campuses, the only reason for paying attention to multicultural and diversity issues was to fulfill federal and accreditation requirements for diversity. Today, we are beginning to see some effort by colleges and universities through programs which promote an inclusive curriculum. For example many colleges and universities now have a program in African Studies, Asian Studies, Latino and Hispanic Studies, Women Studies and Religious Studies.

Higher education institutions, unlike K-12 grade schools have not been held accountable for ensuring the creation of educational climates that promote learning for all its students. In the past decades, institutions of higher education which choose to implement multicultural education have done well in meeting federal compliance requirements related to diversity. As will be discussed late in greater detail, they have also fared well in meeting accreditation requirements on issues related to diversity.

Lack of universal standards related to student learning on U.S. college campuses serves as a confounding factor and account for the limited the enforcement of diversity issues. Many higher education professionals in the U.S. continue to hold the view that there is no direct relationship between academic excellence and an inclusive educational environment even though many of them use inclusive education in their slogans to recruit students from underrepresented populations. Such colleges and universities only consider diversity issues when dealing with federal financial aid requirements. They completely miss the most important goal of higher education: accountability for student learning or "*to promote learning outcomes among all students*" (ACE, 2006). Even though American institutions of higher education serve a very diverse student body, many of those colleges and universities have become fund-generating enterprises rather than being concerned with diversity as a means to promote the success of all students. Many colleges and universities brag about the diverse backgrounds of the students they serve, how many states and countries the students come from without necessarily being concerned about true success and graduation rates among these students.

Regardless of the students' majors, these programs have had great impact on students who take the opportunity to participate in them. In a study conducted with undergraduate and graduate students enrolled in a multicultural education course offered through the Department of Teacher Education in the Burton College of Education at McNeese State University, Ameny-Dixon (2004) found that students' viewed the global perspectives of multicultural education as an eye-opener. It allowed them to discuss personal and interpersonal as well as cultural issues that affected their academic success. It also allowed them to recognize that cultural pluralism is an ideal and healthy state of existence in any productive learning environment. They concluded that it promoted critical thinking and healthy discussions and concluded that multicultural education must be a healthy state in any productive society which cares about respect among existing cultural groups. A review of similar studies showed that the application of the global perspective of multicultural education in teaching and learning practice at institutions of higher education allowed the institutions to become models of democracy for communities in which they are located (AUT/DEA, 1999; Shaw, 2009; Shenker, 1995; Shiel, 2007). In addition to being models for democratic societies:

- Colleges and universities become pillars for academic excellence

- Colleges and universities become models for multicultural societies. Individuals (students, faculty and staff) interacting with each other develop multicultural competence. Students develop critical and problem-solving skills needed for success in the global workplace.
- Colleges and universities become models for an interdependent world, where there is respect for multiple historical perspectives.
- Colleges and universities become places where intercultural consciousness is strengthened, prejudice and all forms of discrimination are reduced, as all members of the learning community develop social and social-action skills.
- Colleges and universities become democratic societies and places where students develop into responsible citizens who care about the state on the nation, the planet, and global dynamics.

Rather than promoting only one way of thinking and one way of life that one cultural group identifies with while despising the ways of life of the other cultural groups, using the global perspective of multicultural education promotes respect and appreciation for intellectual diversity.

Colleges and Universities Become Models for Academic Excellence

The principles and tenets of multicultural education make it possible to promote excellence in performance of all students (Sleeter & Grant, 1999). The fundamental principles of the global perspectives of multicultural education that make it possible to increase academic excellence among diverse groups of students on many campuses in the nation (Green, 1989; Gollnick & Chinn, 2002) include the following:

- Cultural differences have strength and value.
- School and institutions of higher learning should be models for the community in reflecting respect for cultural differences and expression of human rights.
- Social justice and equality for all people should be of paramount importance in the design and delivery of curricula.
- Attitudes and values necessary for the continuation of a democratic society can be promoted in schools and institutions of higher learning.
- Schooling can provide the knowledge, skills, and dispositions for redistribution of power and income among diverse groups of people.
- Educators at institutions of higher learning work with local communities to create an environment that is supportive and respectful of diverse groups of people.

Institutions of higher education whose leaders embrace multicultural education attain high academic standards which benefit all students. Academic excellence begins to matter as these higher education institutions become examples and models for the various K-12 grade public schools and communities in which these institutions are located (Ameny-Dixon, 2004). Can you imagine the impact this would have on the academic standing of our K-12 grade students in the world today compared with students in other parts of the world? Everyone who is familiar with the Trends in International Mathematics and Science Study (TIMSS) conducted by the International Association for the Evaluation of Educational Achievement every four years to assess the achievement of 4th and 8th grades in mathematics and science or the Progress in International Reading Literacy Study (PIRLS) conducted every five years to assess reading achievement of 4th graders worldwide, shows that American students have been performing very poorly in the areas of mathematics, science as well as reading literacy compared to students in the same grades in other parts of the world, and even worse than some of the poor countries of the world. We should be asking ourselves, what are some of the things we need to do right now to reverse this trend if these 4th and 8th graders are to become global leaders tomorrow? (TIMMS & PIRLS, 2011)

Colleges and Universities Are Models of Multicultural Societies

United States is a country which champions equal rights and opportunities for all its citizens and individuals in order to improve the conditions of living for all. Serving as role models for communities and schools, one of our major concerns for institutions of higher education should be to promote democracy through providing equal opportunity for academic and social development and success of all students we serve (Green, 1989). Similar to the 2002 United States Census Bureau, the 2010 U.S. Census predicted that a few years from now nearly one-third of the nation and by the year 2020 nearly one-half of the nation will be composed of minority citizens. This increase in diversity reflects the diversity of our nation and the world (U.S. Census Bureau, 2002). What these statistics means is that there is now a real need more than ever to include minority citizens in the economic, social, and educational mainstream (Gollnick & Chinn, 2002). This reality becomes more apparent on campuses where there is increasing diversity in minority student as well as faculty populations than in those that are less diverse.

Colleges and Universities Become Models of Democratic Societies

The students, faculty, and staff on many campuses in the world including those in the U.S. State today come from various countries. These students, faculty, and staff have various cultural, racial, ethnic, religious, and socio-economic backgrounds. Moreover, today it has become mandatory for universities to admit students and employ faculty from various cultural, racial, ethnic, religious, and socio-economic backgrounds. It has also become mandatory that university communities provide a supportive environment that respects diversity and provide programs that are inclusive for all who are part of it. University administrator and professor should be aware of the various cultural elements in order to be able to provide equitable services.

Colleges and Universities Become Human Right Advocates

College and university administrators and professors at the 2002 National Conference on Multicultural Affairs in Higher Education (Twitty & Mesaric, 2002) reiterated the importance of welcoming diversity on college campuses throughout the nation by highlighting approaches to develop inclusive programs for all students at institutions of higher education. The long-term benefits of the global view of multicultural education greatly outweigh the short-term detriments that usually result from the anxiety experienced by ill-prepared or uninformed educators and administrators (Bennett, 2003; Blair, 2003). Educators begin to develop more adequate understanding of the various cultural elements and how they differ among people from diverse cultures. They begin to have positive ways to relations with persons from other cultures. They will develop programs that motivate diverse student populations (Schulman & Mesa-Bains, 1993).

Educators, students and support staff begin to develop values related to human rights and begin to volunteer more or give more of their time to work on projects that improve human life. In a nation like the United States where beliefs in the assimilation or "the melting-pot" perspective has long been held as the predominant view, educators at institutions of higher education may get confused and stifled by the fast changes going on in the global economy, especially as nations that used to have mediocre economies suddenly become leaders of the global economy. Educators may also wonder why students in these nations are suddenly outcompeting American students, or how the 21st century jobs are filled by college and university graduates from nations that were once referred to as "third-world countries". The answer lies in the simple fact that these graduates are being taught the global perspectives of multicultural education throughout their educational career. In the next chapter, the author discusses how the principles of global perspectives can be used to reinforce the global perspectives to prepare foreign graduates to become global leaders and citizens in the 21st century. For reasons already mentioned, depending on their missions, institutions of higher education are free to select the process they want to use in order to achieve multicultural education and diversity among their faculty, staff, and students.

The challenge for most higher education institutions in the United States is that for a very long time, the assimilation or "melting-pot" perspective of multicultural education was accepted as the predominant perspective of multicultural education. In the 1970's, the concept of pluralism led to the development of the global perspective of multicultural education (Banks, 2005). The American Association for the Advancement of Science (AAAS, 2011), which seeks to "advance science, engineering, and innovation throughout the world for the benefit of all people" has recommended that multicultural education should be promoted in schools and at institutions of Higher Education in order to develop sound science and policy, education and human resources, national and international policies that effect the advancement of science for students at all levels of education. AAAS in *Benchmarks of Science Literacy* (2010) and *Project 2061* emphasized use of multicultural education to create democratic classroom environment in which a multidisciplinary and interdisciplinary curriculum is offered to the students.

The American Council on Education (ACE, 2008) reiterated Gandhi's statement that "the ability to reach unity in diversity will be the beauty and the test of our civilization" and made the following recommendations to colleges and universities which hope to promote democracy, unity, global interconnectedness and human rights:

- Students should learn about the complex relationships between unity and diversity in their local communities, the nation, and the world.
- Students should learn about the ways in which people in their local communities, nation, and the world are increasingly becoming more interdependent with other people around the world and are connected to the economic, political, cultural, environmental and technological changes that are taking place across the planet.
- The teaching of human rights should underpin citizenship education courses and programs in multicultural states and nations.

Sustaining the nation's prosperity in the 21st century will require the appropriate knowledge, skills and attitudes for global work settings. The myth that this can be achieved through the assimilation perspective is discussed in the following Chapter.

CHAPTER 8

THE MYTH THAT THE ASSIMILATION PERSPECTIVE PROMOTES DIVERSITY

For decades, many people including educators in the U.S. have believed that the assimilation or "melting pot" perspective is the best way of developing a shared culture because it allowed the predominant western European/Anglo-Saxon culture to be preserved through the process of acculturation of smaller cultural groups. In the assimilation perspective of multicultural education, to "assimilate" immigrants meant to "Americanize" the immigrants into the predominant western European/Anglo-Saxon culture, by encouraging them to speak the English as the official language.

The assimilation or "melting-pot" perspective required immigrants from smaller cultural groups to denounce their own culture and way of life if they want to be accepted as Americans (McNergney & Hebert, 2001, Castles, 2004). Under this system, smaller cultural groups called "microcultures" were expected to give up their cultural identities in order to blend in or become absorbed by the predominant, western European/Anglo-Saxon mainstream culture or "macroculture" (Bennett, 2003).

The Conceptual Framework of the Assimilation Perspective

In the assimilation perspective of multicultural education, members of the "microcultures" are accepted by the macroculture as part of a "shared culture" once they give up their original identity, values, behavioral styles, languages (including verbal and nonverbal communication styles). Other cultural distinctiveness and identification with other ways of life are viewed as unacceptable, inferior, and a threat to national unity. Everything possible is done by the "popular" culture to suppress the other cultures and to minimize their contributions to the "shared culture" (Bennett, 2003). The initial purpose of assimilation or "melting-pot" perspective was to bring unity through development of a "shared" culture as each microculture become absorbed by the dominant culture. However, it became increasingly difficult to ensure the development of a common "shared" culture because of the dominance by the majority group.

Under the melting-pot or assimilation perspective of multicultural education, the practical and theoretical contributions of the various "microcultures" that are in the minority to the common culture are ignored. The assimilation process is believed to be similar to the mixing of the various cultures in "melting-pot" to create a "mosaic" of a shared American culture.

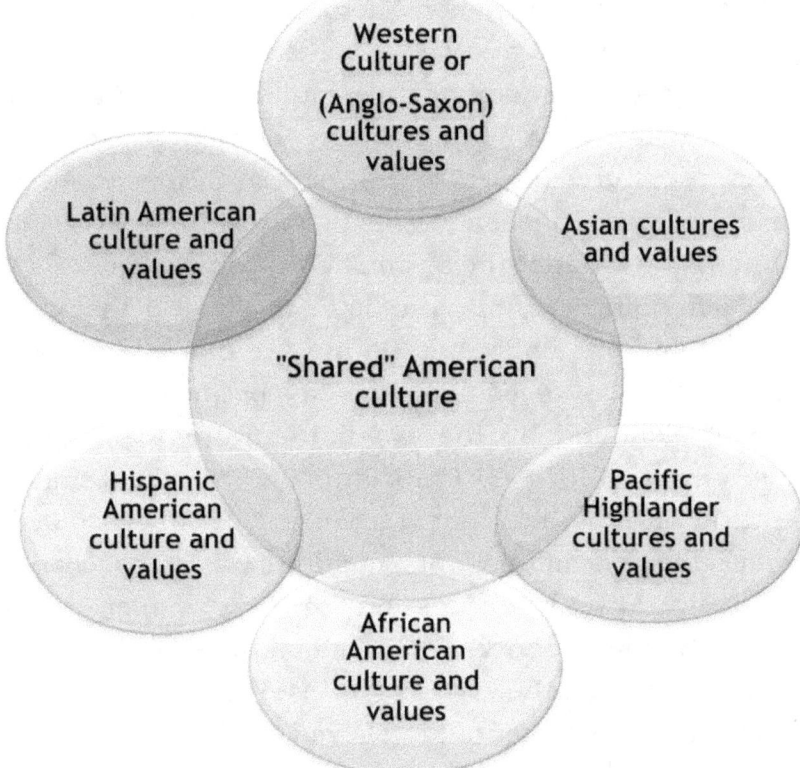

Figure 6: Development of a Core culture through the Assimilation or "Melting Pot" Perspective

Problems with Assimilation Perspective

Although the initial purpose of assimilation or "melting-pot" perspective was to bring unity through development of a common "shared culture" as each "microcultures" becomes absorbed into the mainstream or "macroculture", became very difficult to ensure the development of a common American culture, partly because "microcultures" found it difficult to give up their self-identity and originality. Microcultures did not see the process as a democratic way to achieve equality among all cultural groups. In addition, the resultant common culture was not reflective of all the cultures and values held by the different cultures and favor the Western European Anglo-Saxon culture. It became difficult to identify the various ethnic groups under the assimilation perspective.

"Microcultures" find it difficult to give up their self-identity and originality and do not see this process as a democratic way to achieve equality because everything possible is done by the popular culture to suppress the other cultures. Contributions of the smaller cultural groups are not recognized (Bennett, 2003). Under the assimilation or "melting-pot" perspective of multiculturalism, suppression of the smaller ethnic groups by the majority group leads to a general sense of inequality among the various groups. Figure 6 on page 77 shows the development of a "shared culture" through the assimilation or "melting-pot" perspective.

The resultant common culture in the assimilation perspective is not representative or reflective of all the cultures and values held by the different "microcultures". There is a tendency to favor the Anglo-Saxon or Western-European culture over other minority cultures in spite of the difference in the demographic proportions among the various groups. Assimilation is perceived as acculturation to encourage microcultures to learn the national language and take on social and/or cultural practices of the majority culture.

The need to expand multicultural education beyond the "melting-pot" perspective led to the development of equity pedagogy in public schools as a means of correcting the inequalities in education and among people, particularly, in societies where aspects of human development and values had been neglected. As the world becomes more connected and interdependent, the need to include the global perspective of multicultural education is urgent because in increases awareness of cultural pluralism. Cultural pluralism is an ideal and healthy state in any productive society (Ameny-Dixon, 2004). The next chapter will further discuss the importance of the global perspective of multicultural education. Strong supporters of the assimilation or "melting-pot" perspective have long viewed the introduction of pluralism through the global perspective of multicultural education as a "threat" to the cultural fabric of American culture. They view opposed the global perspective of multicultural education, calling it an assault on western civilization (Sack & Thiel, 1995). Teaching toward social justice requires an adequate understanding student demographics, cultural interactions, race dynamics in the presence of popular culture, and the development of social and social-action skills.

Democratic teaching practices require non-discriminatory learning environment in which myths, stereotypes associated with gender, age, and the various forms of "–isms" are denounced while human values and similarities are appreciated (Nieto, 1996). One should, therefore, ask himself/herself the following questions as he/she thinks about the impact of the assimilation perspective on policy decisions and practices in our educational system. The reader should ask the following questions, considering the fact that we live in the democratic nation of the United States, which was founded by immigrants.

- Does the application of the assimilation perspective help or hurt higher education institutions in the U.S. as we strive to prepare global leaders?
- How beneficial is the assimilation perspective in the preparation of culturally competent graduates and citizens?
- How useful is the assimilation perspective if we are to prepare U.S. graduates to interact comfortably with graduates from other regions of the world?
- In an increasingly interdependent world, will the application of the assimilation perspective provide educators with the most effective method to prepare graduates for the 21st workplace, where they must communicate effectively and compete with graduates from other nations?

CHAPTER 9

THE GLOBAL PERSPECTIVE OF MULTICULTURAL EDUCATION

The global perspective of multicultural education allows people from different cultural backgrounds to respect and appreciate each other's contributions to the wellbeing of individuals in a society, work together toward the wellbeing of the nation and the protection of planet earth.

The Conceptual Framework for the Global Perspective

The conceptual framework for the global perspectives is based on the assumptions that there is shared responsibility among all groups. A major assumption is that people from each group or "microculture" contribute equally to the development of a "shared culture and shared values" regardless of how large or small the group may be (whether it is European-American, Hispanic and Latino American, Asian-American, African-American group).

To promote democracy in a pluralistic society, the notion of acculturation of smaller "microcultures" into the mainstream "macroculture" as was promoted by the assimilation or melting-pot perspective is avoided or minimized. In addition to minimizing discrimination, the global perspective framework is derived from the following four major interactive dimensions.

- Promoting equity pedagogy resulting from self-awareness and awareness of other cultures
- Curriculum reform to develop an inclusive curriculum which presents examples from all cultures to show the contribution of people from all cultural backgrounds to existing knowledge, skills and educational systems
- Teaching for social justice in order to exemplify a democratic society
- Development of multicultural competence by individuals who embrace the global perspectives. Figure 7 on page 83 shows the process by which a shared culture and values is developed as a result of applying the global perspective of culture and value development.

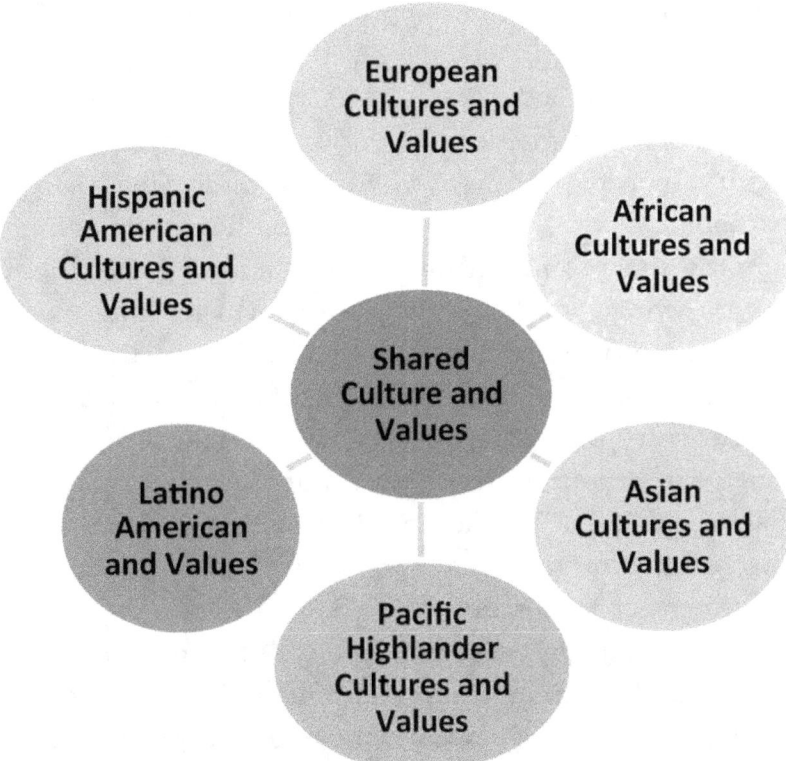

Figure 7: The Development a Shared Culture from the Global Perspective of Multicultural Education (Ameny-Dixon, 2004)

Equity Pedagogy

In American K-12 grade schools, equity pedagogy became an important component of multicultural reform in order to provide equal educational opportunities for all of the nation's children, including socio-economically disadvantaged and ethnic minorities. In addition to the multicultural education approaches used to transform the curriculum (previously discussed in chapter 4), to promote equity pedagogy, teacher preparation programs were required to include curriculum theory and historical inquiry in order to train teachers to minimize biases in the textbooks, media, and other educational materials. It also required use of multiethnic materials in the classrooms. Equity pedagogy attempted to transform the total school environment, paying particular attention to the hidden curriculum and/or differential treatment and expectations of students' performances by school teachers. It also aimed at creating age-appropriate learning activities. Practices related to differential disciplinary policies were closely monitored in order to ensure equal treatment of all students by the teachers.

Equity pedagogy also required that teachers and other educators develop an understanding of their own culture, and an awareness of biases or prejudicial conceptions that may skew their judgment of underrepresented students. Equity pedagogy also advocated that teachers employ alternative instructional strategies to help students with different learning styles.

The development of new professional requirements for teachers, such as pedagogical knowledge and pedagogical content knowledge, appropriate skills and dispositions or attitudes was the result of equity pedagogy. The main goal of equity pedagogy was to allow teachers to adapt alternative teaching methods and modify existing instructional strategies in culturally diverse classrooms in order to ensure the attainment of high academic performance for all students. School and classroom climates were changed; ensuring the least restrictive environment for all students regardless of ethnic, racial, and cultural backgrounds or disabilities.

Curriculum Reform

Curriculum reform has been conducted at U.S. two levels in the U.S. educational system:

- At the elementary and secondary (K-12 grade) school levels
- At the college and university level through teacher education programs

At the college or university level, curriculum reform initiatives have included integration of curriculum theory, curriculum development course, historical inquiry and curriculum analysis in curriculum and instruction programs offered through Colleges of Education. It has also involved inclusion of textbook and instructional media analysis practices to teach future educators about ways to detect cultural biases in textbooks, media, and other educational materials.

At the elementary and secondary (K-12 grade) school levels, curriculum reform has involved increasing the awareness of teachers and school textbook publishers in order to expand traditional course contents and materials used are not primarily mono-ethnic and Anglo-Saxon or European in origin. It serves to include multi-ethnic educational materials in teaching and learning. For most K-12 grade educators, educational reform prompted by the global perspective of multicultural education to produce a pluralistic society required active inquiry and development of new knowledge and understanding of the historical contributions of contemporary and past ethnic groups to the current body of knowledge in the content areas and academic disciplines (Wiles & Brondi, 2002).

Teaching Toward Social Justice

Teaching toward social justice requires adequate understanding of the demographics of the students, culture, and race in popular culture, and development of social action skills. It also emphasizes the clearing up of myths and stereotypes associated with gender, age, and the various races and ethnic groups by stressing basic human similarities (Nieto, 1996).

In addition, teaching toward social justice promotes developing an awareness of the historical roots and an understanding of the evidence of individual and institutional prejudice and discriminations such as cultural racism, sexism, classism, and other forms of prejudice and discrimination. The global perspective of multicultural education goes beyond providing equity education.

- To develop intercultural consciousness which comes only after developing awareness of one's own culture and other person's cultures. Cultural consciousness promotes intercultural and multicultural competence.

- To recognize multiple historical perspectives in order to develop respect for the multiple historical perspectives and contributions of the various cultures to the American educational system.
- To combat all forms of discrimination, including racism, sexism, ageism, classism, and all other forms of prejudice and discrimination including those to persons with disability and to develop appropriate social action skills related to these "– isms"
- To develop core human values - acceptance and appreciation of cultural diversity and respect for human dignity and to develop responsibility to the world community.
- Awareness of the state of planet earth - To increase awareness of the state of the planet and global dynamics, reverence to the earth.

Teaching toward social justice requires adequate understanding of the demographics of the students, culture, and race in popular culture, and development of social action skills. It also emphasizes the clearing up of myths and stereotypes associated with gender, age, and the various race and ethnic groups by stressing basic human similarities (Nieto, 1996). In addition, teaching toward social justice promotes developing an awareness of the historical roots and an understanding of the evidence of individual and institutional prejudice and discriminations such as cultural racism, sexism, classism, and other forms of prejudice and discrimination.

Multicultural Competence

Multicultural competence is a process in which a person understands and appreciates multiple ways of perceiving, evaluating, believing, and solving problems. The person becomes more focused on understanding and learning to negotiate cultural diversity and understanding how this understanding is used to negotiate difficult issues among nations as well as within a single nation with many cultures. Before one can do this, he/she must become aware of his/her own cultural identity and perspectives, and must intentionally and consciously chose to learn about other cultures and perspectives to understand how they are different from his/her own. Multicultural competence is an important foundation for the development of intercultural and cross-cultural interactions and global communications.

Irrespective of the disciplinary areas they are pursuing, college and university graduates require these competencies in order to be able to comfortably interact and communicate with graduates from other nations. To prepare graduates who are competitive on today's global economy, colleges and universities in the U.S. will need to incorporate the global perspectives of multicultural education in the teaching and learning of the various disciplines.

Using the Global Perspective to Develop Global Leaders

The global perspective of multicultural education provide an avenue for students to develop into open-minded citizens who are willing to look beyond their own cultural comfort zones in order to learn from people from other cultures. Students who are in the process of developing multicultural competence begin to care about global issues and exhibit characteristics of global citizens, develop the following characteristics:

- Have strong cultural consciousness and intercultural competence
- Know and appreciate multiple historical perspectives
- Develop the social action skills which allow them to serve as advocates for democracy. They are ready to combat all forms of discrimination to including racism, sexism, ageism, classism, and other forms of prejudice and discrimination
- Develop responsibility to the world community, reverence to the earth, acceptance and appreciation of cultural diversity and respect for human dignity, core human values and human rights
- Develop an awareness of the state of the planet and global dynamics.
- Have recognition of pluralism in a democratic society.

It is not uncommon for students to make the transition from applying the assimilation perspectives to those of the global perspectives of multicultural education as they interact with persons from different cultures and seek solutions to problems and issues which affect all human beings.

Shiel and Mann (2006) recommended that colleges and universities should include specific curricular and extracurricular aspects of higher education including global issues, global processes, internationalization and sustainable social, economic, environmental developments in the preparation of graduates in order to develop global leaders.

- Graduates seek to promote respect and appreciation for others intellectual and cultural backgrounds when working on global issues because they have intercultural consciousness and cross-cultural respect in an increasingly interdependent world.
- Graduates trained as global citizens are less distracted by racial, ethnic, class, language, or other cultural backgrounds that prevent collaborations among nations.
- In a collaborative global arena, graduates develop action skills based on the disciplinary area from which one has received training and their roles and responsibilities in an interdependent world.
- Graduates are aware of the state of their own nation, the planet, and the global dynamics, respect and promote multiple perspectives, appreciate cultural and linguistic diversity within a democratic society, rather than promoting only one way of thinking and one way of life that one cultural group identify with while despising the ways of life of the other cultural groups.
- Graduates are empowered to take advantage of the available resources including intellectual,

cultural, social, resources in solving global issues that impact the state of our planet.
- Graduates become global leaders in the local and global workplace.

Global Perspectives, National and Global Issues

Sheil, Williams and Mann (2005) showed that students develop the following skills that are very important in the development in global leadership:

- "Connected global citizens" who work well as part of a team, recognizing the value and role of each member, inspiring others and developing cross-cultural capability or sensitivity to others.
- Well-rounded graduates with a range of skills which allow graduates to reflect on the global environment in which we operate every day.
- Critical reflectors - graduates challenge knowledge, reflect on the economic, social, and political contexts which shape experience and adopt a critical perspective in analysis and decision-making, reflecting on self and others. They suggested that institutions of higher education should incorporate concepts on the following concepts in order to prepare global leaders:
- Global issues including inequality, injustice and poverty, climate change, global conflicts and human rights.
- Global processes including globalization and types of governance which promote democracy.

- Internationalization including intercultural awareness and communication in an international community.
- Sustainable development in response to social, environmental, economic integration and discussions of precautionary principles.

Shiel and Mann (2006) summarized the characteristics of graduates in terms of global aspects; and summarized them as shown in Figure 8 below.

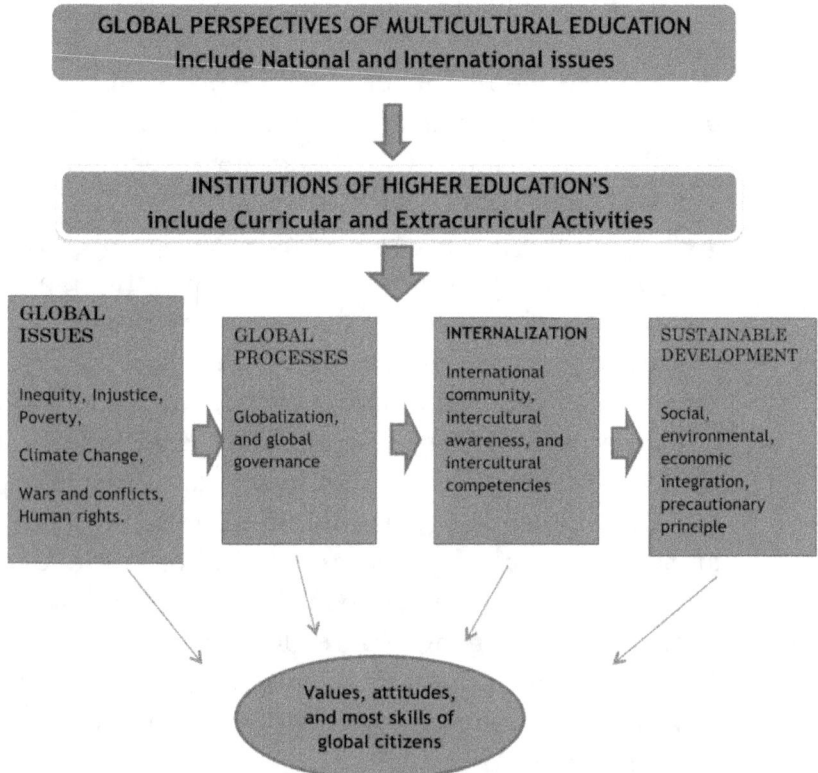

Figure 8: Using the Global Perspectives to Develop Global Citizens. (Adopted from Shiel & Mann, 2006)

Diverse disciplinary areas in the college and university curriculum, should be used as lenses to incorporate global perspectives in all disciplines including history, literature, economics, religion, geography, and the science, technology, engineering, and mathematics (STEM) disciplines to incorporate the key concepts of and principles of global education.

Shaw et al., (1999) conducted workshops for STEM faculty in engineering and veterinary medicine, focusing on issues related to privilege, power, and difference, the team reported very similar results even though each dealt with issues unique to each discipline. Each group of faculty was asked to find out ways they could help their students to think and talk about these issues within each discipline. For example, questions related to veterinary medicine and engineering were generated by the faculty from each discipline. Examples of the issues that questions could address are provided. The reader should excuse the author's bias in selecting issues related to veterinary medicine. Examples of issues that would incorporate the global perspectives of multicultural education during teaching and learning would include the following:

- Climate issues related to changing discipline's changing demographics since women now outnumber men in veterinary practice.
- Impact of poverty on veterinary practice.
- Cultural and gender differences affecting veterinary practice.
- Roles veterinarians play in organizations that help people, posing to allow participants to think and

talk about veterinarians obligations to improve human conditions, e.g. in stopping the spread of zoonotic infections e.g. rabies, swine flu, anthrax, HIN1, West Nile virus, etc.
- Ties veterinarians have with pharmaceutical companies.
- Role veterinarians play during natural disasters, wars, global development.
- Roles veterinarians play in developing legislation about animal welfare.

To expand the discussions, faculty may show why interdisciplinary lenses are important in seeking solutions to global issues, collaborative global projects and issues such global warming, as those students learn why global leadership is needed in the 21st century. Other examples of global or international initiatives that may be used are:

- Aerospace research through the International Space Station
- The Human Genome Project
- Research on renewable energy resources to improve the global economy
- Human Immunodeficiency Virus/Acquired Immunodeficiency Disease Syndrome (HIV/AIDS) research
- Global collaboration and interdiction to reduce terrorism

The goal of preparing global leaders through American institutions of higher education via application of the global perspectives and principles of multicultural education and through globalization can be achieved using diverse disciplinary lenses, including history, literature, economics, religion, geography, and the science, technology, engineering, and mathematics (STEM) disciplinary areas. It should, however, be remembered the true measure of attainment of the global outcomes are in the knowledge, skills and attitudes exhibited by the graduates as they become global leaders.

Considering the fact that the world is becoming smaller and more interdependent, the reader should ask himself/herself the following questions:

- How can institutions of higher education in the U.S. use the global perspective of multicultural education to facilitate the preparation of global leaders?
- How beneficial is the global perspective of multicultural education to higher education institutions as they strive to prepare students who are culturally competent and value democracy?
- With the world becoming more interdependent, how can colleges and universities utilize the principles of the global perspective of multicultural education to prepare graduates with 21st century skills, including intercultural communication skills and graduates who can outcompete their counterparts from other nations?

CHAPTER 10

NEW ROLES INSTITUTION OF HIGHER EDUCATION MUST ASSUME TO PREPARE GLOBAL LEADERS

Higher education has always played a major role in equipping students with the skills, knowledge and attitudes they need to be successful in society. However, in today's global economy, this success needs to include success in the global workplace. While it seems American institutions of higher education are not ready to "boldly embrace" the global perspectives multicultural education, as indicated in the title of this book, *Transforming Higher Education to Prepare Global Leaders: Is Higher Education Ready for the Global Perspectives of Multicultural Education?*, the 21st century global economy is not giving institutions any more time to sit back and watch their graduates outcompeted by those from other countries (Wang & Olsen, 2009; Rhoads &Szelenyi, 2011; Rubin, 2009).

As a Global Leader Each Institution of Higher Education Must Promote Multicultural and Global Education

Higher education institutions must include preparation of global leaders in their missions and find ways to fulfill these missions. They must find ways to make multicultural education work if they are to stay open and prepare graduates who are competitive in the 21st century workplace (Smith, 2009; Twitty & Mesaric, 2002). Colleges and universities and educators at these institutions need to have the courage to overcome myths originating from the assimilation perspective, which have led to the opposition of the global perspective of multicultural education (Sack & Thiel, 1995).

Banks et al. (2005) identified the following concepts and principles which should be incorporated into the college of university curriculum in order to promote an understanding of the global perspective of multicultural education:

- Democracy
- Diversity
- Globalization
- Sustainable development
- Empire
- Imperialism

- Power
- Prejudice
- Discrimination
- Racism
- Migration
- Identity/Diversity
- Multiple Perspectives
- Patriotism
- Cosmopolitism

After students are taught these concepts they should have the foundation for understanding global perspective of multicultural education so that they can make the transition to understanding globalization and internationalization. It is suggested that before sending students abroad for 1-2 weeks travel excursions expecting these to change students' knowledge, skills, and attitudes about other cultures, as is commonly done by most U.S. colleges and universities, students should be taught the application of the global perspective of multicultural education. These applications should be taught or discussed before students are sent far away on long international trips. In addition to the above multicultural education concepts, Banks (2005) suggested that the following methods should be used:

- Students should learn about complex relationships between unity and diversity in their local communities, the nation, and the world the world
- Students should learn about the ways in which people in their community, nation, and region are increasingly interdependent with other

other people around the world and are connected to the economic, political, cultural, environmental, and technological changes taking place across the planet.
- The teaching of human rights should underpin citizenship education courses and programs in multicultural nation-states.
- Students should be taught knowledge about democracy and democratic institutions and provide opportunities to practice democracy.

U.S. should develop global perspective programs similar to those used by European higher educators (AUT/DEA, 1999; Shiel & Mann, 2006) in order to reverse trends which have kept American higher education and its graduates behind while European and Asian graduates excel in the 21st century global workplace. Incorporating the global perspective of multicultural education into their educational system has allowed higher educators in these countries to find common ground to work together to prepare graduates who will become global leaders (Cortes, 1998; Iwata, 2004; Olsen & Shoenberg, 2007).

Job outsourcing continues to make other countries stronger economically while the U.S. national economy seems to keep getting weaker (Sanderson, 2011), partly because Chinese graduates have a more impressive technological know-how than U.S. graduates. China also has tremendous manufacturing capacity with companies from the U.S., Japan and Europe, which are eager to share in penetrating some of the Chinese technology manufacturing markets. These Chinese graduates can interact freely with people from other parts of the world, learn their culture, language, values and have risen to become leaders in today's global economy. Secondly, Chinese have highly skilled graduates who are paid 30 times lower than U.S. graduates (Haycook, 2006). These Chinese and foreign graduates are filling top positions in major industries in the United States and other regions of the world (Shiel, et al., 2005). This phenomenon shows the urgency to increase the number of U.S. graduates with 21st century skills as described in the Partnerships for Century Skills (2009a).

Assuming the Role of a *Communiversity* Each Institution of Higher Education Should Promote Civic Engagement

U.S. colleges and universities also need to prepare graduates who are civic and global leaders. This is an important step towards global leadership. In a collaborative project between the Global Perspective Institute and the American Association of Colleges and Universities (AACU), funded by the U.S. Department of Education, involving 60 higher education institutions, thirty civic organizations, eleven private and government foundations, fourteen higher education associations and twelve disciplinary associations, civic learning and democratic engagement projects were used to demonstrate that the following themes:

- A holistic view of student learning, promoted by multicultural education teaches students how to view themselves (their values and motivation),

think and act (knowledge and skills) and how to relate to others in their communities.
- Holistic learning through hands-on engagement prepares students for work and citizenship.
- A learning environment which fosters civic learning and democratic engagement is a diverse one composed of people from various racial cultural and socioeconomic backgrounds.
- For civic learning to be part of the landscape of American Higher Education, "it must be a central, rather than marginal, institutionalized rather than fragmented" (Jacoby et al. 2009).
- For civic learning to be part of the landscape of American Higher Education, it must be an integral part of the institution rather than something that students encounter haphazardly through the curriculum and co-curriculum"
- For civic learning to be part of the landscape of American Higher Education, it must become a key component of institutional identity, with faculty deeply involved in creating engaged academic communities that reflect and model democratic values.

While this study used a model similar to that of a communiversity, and demonstrated the power of multicultural education in facilitating civic engagement, colleges and universities should include the global perspective of multicultural education in order to promote the preparation of global leaders because colleges and universities are increasingly composed of diverse groups of people from different nations and cultural backgrounds working together as part of a global learning community (Suarez-Orozco & Quin-Hilliard, 2004).

College and university curricula at the general education core and discipline levels must be transformed as well. Educators who support multicultural education report that transforming the higher education curriculum has great impact on students, institutions and the society at large. Kogler and Stueber (1999) found that multicultural education advances cognitive capabilities and enables students to understand different cultural perspectives when solving problems. They also found that it allows students to develop a reflexive understanding of how they represent concepts and structures shared by individuals in different experiential contexts.

Similar results were reported following simulation studies involving multicultural education, where students were assessed on essential cognitive mechanisms such as perspective-taking, language acquisition, and situated rationality. Reflexive perspective-taking helped students to come to a more pluralistic and open-minded worldview. Recent studies in cognitive science supported these results and showed that application of multicultural education taught students essential cognitive mechanisms that were very important in developing intelligence. Students were more willing to accept the complexities and richness of human social and emotional intelligence (Solovey & Mayer, 1990).

Assuming the Role of a *Pluriversity* Each Institution of Higher Education Should Promote Global Engagement and Global Leadership

As nations increasingly work together to find solution to global issues related to the ecosystem, nuclear weapons, terrorism, human rights, and scarce national resources, applying the global perspectives of multicultural education allows them to focus on solutions by considering the democratic values, cultural diversity, national, and common interests rather than focusing on differences.

Olsen et al. (2007) described common goals and learning outcomes for the global principles of multicultural education and internationalization. Using the shared global values and shared challenges, the shared nature of the work, and they identified the following shared outcomes:

- Global knowledge.
    - Knowledge of the world through diverse disciplinary lenses, including history, literature, economics, religion, geography, and the science, technology, engineering and mathematics (STEM) disciplines.
    - Knowledge of the interconnectedness of world systems, including sustainability, and social justice, and global forces.
    - Knowledge of culture and how culture affects personal, national, and international relations.

- Global perspective consciousness and intercultural sensitivity.
    - Recognition that one's view of the world is not universally shared.
    - Recognition that others may have profoundly different perspectives.
    - Ability to perceive any given event from more than one cultural viewpoint.

- Global intercultural communication skills.
    - Appreciation of competence a second language (or in two or more languages).
    - Ability to interact successfully with people of other cultures.
    - Ability to gather information from multiple sources, using multiple mechanisms, including technology.

Before one can grasp globalization issues, he/she must have a good understanding of domestic issues within the U.S. including cultural, social, racial and ethnic issues that affect our educational system or national economy through an understanding of multicultural education. On the other hand, internationalization focuses on knowledge of cultures outside the United States. Globalization becomes a process which institutions in the U.S. can use to make the transition from multicultural education to internationalization.

Institutions of higher education in the United States and in other parts of the world today have a culturally diverse student body, and a diverse faculty and staff population. This cultural pluralism makes Colleges and Universities the "niche" for developing global learning communities in the 21st century. Most institutions of higher education already have international faculty and international students in their campus communities. Many colleges and universities also have international student exchange programs which reinforce global curricular and extracurricular programs.

Major colleges and universities in the U.S. and Europe have started using the *communiversity* and *pluriversity* models and research to determine if graduates are developing multiple historical perspectives, strong intercultural consciousness, or a reduced level of prejudice towards people from other cultures, and if they can work well with others with different national and cultural backgrounds after the students they have completed various levels of global education through the college or university curriculum (AUD/DEA, 1999; Shiel et al., 2005). Graduates are assessed through completion of global projects to determine if they have developed characteristics which will allow them to serve successfully as leaders in the global marketplace (Shiel, 2007).

New Roles for Colleges and Universities in the U.S.

Institutions of higher education or colleges and universities in the U.S. should have the following new roles:

- Educators at institutions of higher education must have a thorough understanding of the global perspectives and principles of multicultural education in order to facilitate these new roles. They must have the courage to challenge long-held misconceptions about multicultural education in order to incorporate the global perspectives in the teaching of every discipline as they prepare global leaders.
- Colleges and universities should become models for "global learning communities", using the concept of global citizenship as a framework, to lead and spearhead the education of global leaders.
- Colleges and universities should become models for "global learning communities", using the concept of global citizenship as a framework, to lead and spearhead the education of global leaders.
- Colleges and universities should prepare graduates with global knowledge, global consciousness and intercultural communication skills
- Colleges and universities should become centers of educational excellence to promote the quality of the American educational system rather than the revenue generating enterprises they are today.
- Colleges and universities should serve their communities by behaving like responsible model citizens in their own right; as organizations which consider the impact of their daily operations on the environment.
- Colleges and universities should be responsible for curriculum offered through their campuses

and the pedagogy of methods of teaching used in the classrooms, making sure that the global perspectives of multicultural education is incorporated in every discipline and students and taught how to use these principles critically to solve social, economic, environmental and related global problems as they are prepared to become global leaders.
- Colleges and universities should become responsible for providing extracurricular activities which support multicultural education, global citizenship and international awareness.
- Colleges and universities should expand their roles from serving as a "*communiversity*" working with other universities in the country and concerned only with domestic issues in their communities to serving as a "*pluriversity*" working by with universities abroad in order to produce leaders for the 21st century global economy.

Finally, even though there is no centralized control of the higher education curriculum as in European, Asian and other countries, the United States Department of Education should provide some guidelines on what is considered college- or university-level learning in order to promote academic quality and prevent the proliferation of "online diploma mills". To prepare global leaders, there should be a redesign of programs provided to college and university students so that 21st century skills, the global perspectives of multicultural education and internationalization are included in all aspects of college-level learning. Accountability requirements in American higher education should include diversity and intercultural communications.

The urgency for American institutions of higher education to be ready or have the courage to serve new roles as leaders must be met now if these institutions are to serve as models of global communities, centers for educational excellence, models of democratic values and human rights, and models for the public and private K-12 schools and communities in which they are located. The urgency is now if these institutions are to produce graduates who are global leaders in the 21st century.

REFERENCES

American Association for the Advancement of Science. (1989). *Science for All Americans*. New York: Oxford University Press.

American Association for the Advancement of Science *(2009) Project 2061*. New York: Oxford University Press.

American Association for the Advancement of Science (2010). *Benchmarks of Science Literacy (2010)*. New York: Oxford University Press.

American Council on Education. (2004). *Putting College Costs in Context*. Available online at www.acenet.edu/bookstore/pdf/2004_college_costs.pdf.

American Council on Education. (2006). *Democracy and Diversity: Principles and Concepts for Educating Citizens in a Global Age"*. Published by the American Council on Education.

American Council on Education. (2007). *At Home in the World: Bridging the Gap Between Internationalization and Multicultural Education.* Published by the American Council on Education as the Global Learning for All: Fourth in a Series of Working Papers on Internationalizing Higher Education in the Unites States.

The American Council on Education. (2008). *Preparing Leaders for the Future: A Toolkit for Developing Administrators in Higher Education.* A publication of the ACE Center for Advancement of Racial and Ethnic Equity. Available online at www.acenet.edu/content/navigationmenu/programsServices/Care

Ameny-Dixon, G.M. (2004). *Why Multicultural is More Important in Higher Education Now than Ever: A Global Perspective.* McNeese State University. Retrieved on November 10, 2011 from http://www.nationalforum.com.

Austin, A. W. & Austin, H. S. (2000). *Leadership reconsidered: Engaging higher education in social change.* Battle Creek., MI: W. K. Kellogg Foundation.

AUT/DEA (1999). *Globalization and Higher Education: Guidelines on Ethical Issues Arising from International Academic Activities.* London: AUT/DEA

Author, D. H., Levy, F., & Murnane, R. J. (2003). The skill content of recent technological change: An empirical exploration. *Quarterly Journal of Economics, 118 (4),*
1279-1333.

Banks, J.A. (1987). *Teaching strategies for ethnic studies* (4th ed.). Boston: Allyn and Bacon, Inc.

References

Banks, J.A. & Banks, C. M. A. (1993). *Multicultural Education: Issues and Perspectives (2nd Ed.)*. Boston: Allyn and Bacon: A Division of Simon and Schuster, Inc.

Banks, J.A. & Banks, C. M. A. (1997). *Multicultural Education Issues and Perspectives*. (3rd Ed.). Needham Heights, MA: Allyn and Bacon.

Banks, J. A. (1999). *Introduction to Multicultural Education*. (2nd Ed.). Boston: Allyn Bacon. Retrieved on November 12, 2011 from www.intime.uni.edu/multicultural/curriculum/aproachs.htm.

Banks, J. A. (2002). *Multicultural Education: Issues and Perspectives*. Boston: Jossey Bass.

Banks, J.A., Cookson, P., Gay, G., Hawley, W. D., Irvine, J. J., Nieto, S. & Stephan, W. G. (2001). *Diversity Within Unity: Essential Principles for Teaching in a Multicultural Society*. The Phi Delta Kappan, Vol. 83, No. 3, Nov 2001. Retrieved November 5, 2011 from www.jstor.org/pss/20440100

Banks J. A. & McGee C. A., et al. (2005). Democracy and Diversity: Principles and Concepts for Educating Citizens in a Global Age. Published by the Center for Multicultural Education, College of Education. University of Washington, Seattle. Retrieved on November 5, 2011 from the website www.depts.washington.edu/centerme/demDiv.pdf.

Barkan, E. (2005). History on the line: Engaging history, managing conflict and reconciliation. *History Workshop Journal 59*, 301-308.

Bellanca J. & Bradt, R, (2010 Ed.). *21st Century Skills: Rethinking How Students Learn*. Solutions Tree Press.

Bennett, C.I. (1999). *Comprehensive Multicultural Education: Theory and Practice*. Needham Heights, MA: Allyn and Bacon.

Bennett, C.I. (2003). *Comprehensive multicultural education: Theory and practice*. Boston: Pearson Education, Inc.

Blair, T.R. (2003). *New teacher's performance-based guide to culturally diverse classrooms*. Boston: Pearson Education, Inc.

Boise, R. (1993). *Early turning points in professional careers of women and minorities. New Directions for Teaching and Learning, 53,* 71-79.

Braskamp, L. A. (2011). Higher Education for Civic Learning and Democratic Engagement: Reinvesting in Longstanding Commitments. *Diversity & Democracy Volume 14,* Number 3.

Brown, W. (2006). *Regulating aversion: Tolerance in the age of identity and empire*. Princeton, NJ: Princeton University Press.

Bruner, J. (2006). *The Culture of Education*. Harvard University Press: Cambridge, MA

Castles, S. (2004). Migration, Citizenship, and Education. In *Diversity and Citizenship Education: Global Perspectives* edited by James A. Banks (2004). Jossey-Bass. A Wiley & Sons, San Francisco, CA.

Champagnes, D. (2005). Rethinking native relations with contemporary nation states. In D. Champagne, K. J. Torjesen, & S. Steiner (Eds.), *Indigenous people and the modern state* (pp3-23). Walnut Creek, CA: Alta Vista Press.

Clark, C., & Gorski, P. (2002). *Multicultural education and the digital divide: Focus on socioeconomic class background. Multicultural Perspectives, 4(3)*, 25-36.

Combs, G. M. (2002). Meeting the leadership challenge of a diverse and pluralistic workplace: Implications of self-efficacy for diversity training. *Journal of Leadership and Organizational Studies, 8(4)*, 1-16.

Cortes, C.E. (1998). Global Education and Multicultural Education. Towards a 21st Century Intersection. In L. Swatz, L. Warner, & D. L. Grossman (eds.) *Intersections: A professional development project in multicultural education and global education, Asian and American studies.* Boston: The Children's Museum, pp. 144-133.

Cushner, K., McClelland A., & Safford, P. (2000). *Human diversity in education: An integrative approach (3rd Ed.).* Boston: McGraw Hill.

Duhon, G., Mundy, M., Leder, S., LeBert, L., & Ameny-Dixon, G. (2002). *Addressing racism in the classroom: Using a case studies approach.* Conference and program proceedings of the National Conference on Multicultural Affairs in Higher Education, San Antonio, TX.

Duhon-Boudreau, G. (1998). *An interdisciplinary approach to issues and practices in teacher education.* Lewiston, NY: The Edwin-Mellen Press.

Gardner H. 1983. Frames of mind: The theory of multiple intelligences. New York: NY Basic Books.

Gladdwell, M. (2000). *The tipping point: How little things can make a big difference.* Boston: Little, Brown.

Green, M.F. (1989). *Minorities on campus: A handbook for enhancing diversity.* Washington DC: American Council on Education.

Greenleaf, R. K. (2002). The Servant Leader Within: *A Journey into the Nature of Legitimate Power and Greatness* (25th anniversary ed.). New York: Paulist Press. Retrieved on November 18th, 2011 from www.greenleaf.org/

Gollnick, D.M., & Chinn, P.C. (2002). *Multicultural education in a pluralistic society (6th Ed.).* Upper Saddle River, NJ: Pearson Education Inc.

Giroux, H. A. (1998). The politics of national identity and the pedagogy of multiculturalism in the USA. In D. Bennett (ed.), *Multicultural states: Rethinking differences and identity.* (pp. 178-194). New York: Routledge.

Gupta, A. (2006). *Affirmative action in higher education in India and the US: A study of contrast.* (Research and Occasional Papers Series, CSHE.10.06), Berkeley: University of California, Berkeley, and Center for Studies in Higher Education.

Gutman, A. & Thompson, D. (2004). Why deliberate democracy? Princeton, NJ: Princeton University Press.

Haycock, K. (2006). *Promise abandoned: How policy choices and institutional practices restrict college opportunities.* Washington, D.C.: Education Trust.

HLC (2003). *The Higher Learning Commission's Statement on Diversity.* Available online at ncahlc.org/hlcdiversitystament2003.doc/

Hirsh, E.D. (1987). Cultural literacy: *What every American needs to know.* Boston: Houghton-Mifflin.

International Institute for Management Development. (2009). IMD competitiveness yearbook. Lausanne, Switzerland: Author.

Iwata, K. (2004). *The power of diversity: 5 essential competencies for leading a diverse workforce.* Petaluma, CA: Global Insight Publishing.

Jacoby, B. and Associates (2009). Civic Engagement in Higher Education: Concepts and Practices. Jossey Bass Higher Education and Adult Education. San Francisco, CA.

Johnson, D.W., & Johnson, R.T. (2002). *Multicultural education and human relations: Valuing diversity.* Boston: Allyn and Bacon.

Kogler, H. and Stueber, K. (2000). Empathy and Urgency: The Problem of Understanding the Human Mind. Westview Press.

Larson, C.L., & Ovando, C.J. (2001). *The color of bureaucracy: The politics of equity in multicultural school communities.* Belmont, CA: Thomson Learning, Inc.

Layer, G. (Ed.). (2005). *Closing the equity gap: The impact of widening participation strategies in the UK and USA.* Leicester, UK: National Institute of Adult Continuing Education.

Levy, J. (1997). The VENN view of diversity: Understanding differences through similarities. Retrieved from www.iteachnet.com/April97/VennDiversity.htm

Lorenz, D. (2011). How the World Became Smaller: From Pigeon Post to the Internet. *History Today, Volume 61, Issue 11,* November 2011. Retrieved from www.questia.com/googlescholar.qst?docld=5001639477

Marginson, S. (2011). The Rise of the Global University: 5 New Tensions. *Chronicles of Higher Education*. Retrieved from http://chronicle.com

McNergney, R.F., & Hebert, J.M. (2001). *Foundations of education: The challenge of professional practice*. Boston: Allyn and Bacon.

Merryfield, M. M. (1996). Making Connections between multicultural and global education. Washington, DC: American Association of Colleges for Teacher Education.

Nieto, S. (1996). *Affirming diversity: The sociopolitical context of multicultural education (2nd Ed.)*. White Plains, NY: Longman Publishers.

NCATE (2006). The National Committee for the Accreditation of Teacher Education (NCATE) – Standard 4: Diversity. Available online at www.ncate.org/Public/Newsroom/NCATENewsPress Release

Olsen, C. L., Evans, R. & Shoenberg, R. F. (2007). *At Home in the World: Bridging the Gap between Internationalization and Multicultural Education"*. Global Learning for All: The Fourth in a Series of Working Papers on Internationalizing Higher Education in the United States. Published by the American Council on Education.

Suarez-Orozco, M. M. & Quin-Hilliard, D. B. (2004). *Globalization: Culture and Education in the New Millennium*. University of California Press.

Ottoman, S. (2004). *Trade: Outsourcing Jobs*. Retrieved October 15, 2011 from www.cfr.org/pakistan/trade-outsourcing-jobs/p7749.

Oxfam Great Britain (2006). *Education for global citizenship: A guide for schools.* Available from http://oxfam.org.uk/education/gc/files/education-for_global_ citizenship_ a_ guide_ for_ schools.pdf

Pang, V.O. (2001). *Multicultural education: A caring-centered, reflective approach.* New York: McGraw-Hill.

Partnership for 21st Century Skills. (2009a). *Framework for 21st Century Learning.* Tucson, AZ: Author. Available at www.21stcenturyskills.org/documents/ framework_flyer_updated_april_2009.pdf

Partnership for 21st Century Skills. (2009b). *The Mile Guide: Milestones for improving learning and education.* Tucson, AZ: Author. Available at www.21stcenturyskills. org/documents/mile_guide_091101.pdf.

Perlman, J. & Waters, M. C. (Eds.). (2002). *The new race question: How the census counts multicultural individuals.* New York: Russell Sage Foundation.

Quicksey, A. (2009). *Smaller World, Bigger Impact: Using Technology and social media to create change on a larger scale.* Retrieved November 2, 2011 from http://blog.orgsync.com/2009/social-justice/

Quiseberry, N.L., McIntyre D.J., & Duhon, G.M. (2002). *Racism in the classroom: Case studies.* A Joint Publication of the Association of Teacher Educators and Association for Childhood Education International, Olney, MD.

Rhoads, R.A. & Szelenyi, K. (2011). *Global Citizenship and the University: Advancing Social Life and Relations in an Interdependent World.* Stanford University Press.

Rubin, J. (2009). *Why Your World is About to Get a Whole Lot Smaller: Oil and the End of Globalization.* Random House Publishing Group, Inc. New York.

Sacks, D. O. & Thiel, P. A. (1995). *The Diversity Myth: Multiculturalism and the Politics of Intolerance at Stanford.* Published by the Independent Institute, 134 Ninety Eighth Avenue, Oakland, CA 94603.

SACS-COC (2003). The Southern Association of Colleges and Schools, Commission on Colleges. *Diversity: a Position Statement.* Available online at www.sacscoc.org/documents/DiversityStatement.pdf

Sanderson, J. (2011). *American Job Outsourcing: Making other countries a lot stronger.* Retrieved from http://www.politicususa.com/en/american-job-outsourcing-making-other-coutries-a-lot-stronger (Published Feb 27, 2011).

Scott, M. (2009). Competitiveness: The U.S. and Europe are tops. *Business Week.* Accessed at www.businessweek.com/globalbiz/content/may2009/gb20090519_222765.htm.

Shaw, S. M., Amico, R., & Champeau. D. (2009). Teaching Diversity and Democracy across the disciplines: Who, What, and How. *Diversity and Democracy Volume 12*, Number 3. Retrieved on November 18, 2011 from www.diversityweb.org/DiversityDemocracy/vol12no3.pdf

Shaw, S. M., Amico, R., & Champeau. D. (2009). *Infusing Diversity in the Sciences and Professional Disciplines. Diversity and Democracy,* Volume 12, Number 4. Retrieved on November 18, 2011 from www.diversityweb.org/DiversityDemocracy/vol12no3/shaw.cfm

Shenker, O. (1995). Global Perspectives on Human Resource Management. New York: Prentice Hall.

Sheil, C., Williams, A. & Mann S. (2005). Global Perspectives and Sustainable Development in the Curriculum: Enhanced Employability, More Thoughtful Society? In *Enhancing graduate employability: The roles of learning, teaching, research and knowledge transfer.* Proceedings of the Bournemouth University Learning and Teaching Conference.

Shiel, C. (2007). Developing global citizens: The way forward. *The International Journal of Learning, 14 (4),* 153-167.

Short, D. (2003). Reconciliation, assimilation, and the indigenous peoples of Australia. International Political Science Review, 24 (4), 491-513.

Shulman, J., & Mesa-Bains, H. (1993). *Diversity in the classroom: A casebook for teachers and teacher educators.* Hillsdale, NJ: Lawrence Erlbaum Associates, Inc.

Silverman, R., Welty, W., & Lyon, S. (1994). *Multicultural education cases for teacher problem solving.* Boston: McGraw-Hill Inc.

Slaughter, J. B. (2004). Diversity and Equity in Higher Education: A new paradigm for institutional excellence. Speech given November 1, 2004, John Hopkins University, Baltimore

Sleeter, C.E., & Grant, C.A. (1999). *Making choices for multicultural education: Five approaches to race, class, and gender (3rd Ed.).* Upper Saddle River, NJ: Prentice Hall.

Smith, D. G. (2009), Diversity's Promise for Higher Education: Making it Work. The John Hopkins University Press.

Solovey, P. & Mayer, J. D. (1990). Emotional intelligence, imagination, Cognition and Personality pp.185-211.

Sumida, S. & Gurin, P. A. (2001). Celebration of power. In D. L. Schoem & S. Hurtado (Eds.), Intergroup dialogue: Deliberate democracy in school, college community, and workplace (pp.280-293). Ann Arbor: University of Michigan.

TIMMS & PIRLS, (2011). *Trends in International Mathematics and Science Study and Progress in International Reading Literacy Study.* Retrieved on November 14, 2011 from http://www.timss.org/

Twitty, J.R., & Mesaric, T.C. (2002). *The importance of welcoming diversity on college campuses.* Program and Conference Proceedings of the National Conference on Multicultural Affairs in Higher Education, October 20-23, 2002. San Antonio, Texas.

United States Census Bureau. (2010). *Press release on minority populations in the United States. at the end of the year 2010.* Retrieved on October 28, 2011 from http://2010.census.gov/2010census/

van Ark B., Barrington, L. Fosler, G. Hulten, C. & Woock, C. (2009). *Innovation and U.S. competiveness: Reevaluating the contributors to growth.* New York: The Conference Board.

Wang, H. & Olson, N. (2009). A Journey to Unlearn and Learn in Multicultural Education (Eds.). In Peter Lang, 2009.

Western Association of Schools and Colleges (2002). A guide to using evidence in the accreditation process. Oakland:, CA: Author.

White, S. & Johnson, L. (2006). Tolerance in teacher education: restructuring the curriculum in a diverse but segregated university classroom. *Multicultural Education: Issues and Perspectives, Volume 13*, Issue 3.

Wiles, J., & Brondi, J. (2002). *Curriculum development: A guide to practice (6th Ed).* Upper Saddle River, NJ: Pearson Education.

INDEX

21st century, 9, 12, 15-16, 30, 38, 42, 73-74, 94, 97, 106, 108-109

   jobs, 73

   skills, ix, 7,11, 13, 17-18, 95, 101, 108

   workplace, 6-7, 15, 98, 100

A

academic excellence, 31, 66-69

Access and Equity, 29-30

Accountability, 3, 13, 26, 29-32, 50, 65-66, 109

affirmative action, 5

Affordability, 29-30

Ameny-Dixon, G. M., v-vii, ix-x, 4, 8, 10, 53; 59-60, 67, 70, 79, 83, 112, 115

American Association for the Advancement of Science (AAAS), 57, 73

American Council on Education (ACE), 1, 26-27, 30, 33, 57, 66, 74

Amico, R., 120

Anglo-Saxon culture. *See* cultures: Anglo-Saxon

assimilation perspective. *See* perspectives: assimilation

Austin, A. W., 5, 112

Austin, H. S., 5, 112

Autor, D. H., 17, 112

B

Banks, C. M. A., 57, 113

Banks, J. A., 3, 22, 55, 56-57, 60, 73, 98-99, 112-114

Barkan, E., 5, 113

Barrington, L., 122

Bellanca, J., 16-17, 113

Bennett, C. I., 53, 72, 76, 78, 114, 116

Blair, T. R., 72, 114

Boise, R., 57, 114

Bradt, R, 16-17, 113

Braskamp, L. A., 114

Brondi, J., 86, 123

Brown, W., 4, 114

Bruner, J., 39, 114

C

Carnegie System of credits, 27

Castles, S., 76, 114

Champagnes, D., 114

Champeau, D., 120

China, 18-19, 21, 100

Chinn, P. C., 53, 69, 71, 116

civic engagement, 9, 101-102

Clark, C., 57, 115

Combs, G. M., 7, 115

Commission on Independent Colleges and Universities (CICU), 33

communication, 12, 17, 21, 48, 50, 76, 92, 95, 107

communiversity, 9-10, 13, 29, 101-102, 106, 108

Cookson, P., 113

Cortes, C. E., 20, 100, 115

Council for Higher Education Accreditation (CHEA), 32-33

cultures

 Anglo-Saxon, 56, 75-76, 78, 85

 European, 42-43

 shared culture, 64, 75-78, 81-83

curriculum. *See also* K-12: curriculum

 reform, 55, 64, 82, 85

Cushner, K., 57, 115

D

democracy, 5-6, 9, 22, 60-61, 67, 70, 74, 82, 89, 91, 95, 98, 100

democratic society, 4, 63, 69, 82, 89-90

discrimination, 5, 54, 60, 68, 82, 86-87, 89, 99

diversity, vii, 2-4, 6-7, 16, 18, 21-24, 33, 40, 49, 56-58, 60-66, 68, 71-75, 87-90, 98-99, 104, 109

 myth, 21

Duhon, G. M., 53, 57, 115, 119

Duhon-Boudreau, G., 57, 115

E

economy, ix, 16, 18-20, 29, 36, 105

   U.S., 16, 19, 100

equity pedagogy, 59, 79, 82-84

Europe, 100, 106

Evans, R., 118

F

Facebook, 36-37, 40

Finland, 21

Fosler, G., 122

Framework, 7, 11, 13, 76, 81-82, 107

G

Gandhi, 74

Gardner, H., 115

Gay, G., 113

Germany, 18

Giroux, H. A., 116

Gladdwell, M., 115

global

   citizen(s)(-ship), 4, 8, 20, 41, 47, 49, 51, 59, 89-92, 107-108

   communication, 23, 39-40, 105

   communities, x, 20, 40-42, 45-48, 50, 109

   competition, 18

connectedness, 51

economy, x, 16, 18, 21, 72, 88, 94, 97, 101, 108

engagement, 104

knowledge, 23, 50, 104, 107

leaders, x, 1-3, 6, 8, 10, 13, 16, 21, 23-24, 30, 51, 59, 70, 73, 88, 91, 94-95, 97-98, 100-102, 104, 107-109

learning communities, 8, 46, 49, 50, 103, 106-107

global perspective. *See* perspectives: global

Global Perspective Institute and the American Association of Colleges and Universities (AACU), 101

global village, 35, 40, 42-45, 47

Gollnick, D. M., 53, 69, 71, 116

Gorski, P., 57, 115

graduate(s), ix-x, 2, 4, 6, 8-11, 13, 15-21, 24, 29-30, 42, 48-49, 59, 73, 80, 88, 90-92, 95, 98, 100-101, 106-107, 109

Grant, C. A., 69, 121

Green, M. F., 69, 71, 116

Greenleaf, R. K., 116

Gupta, A., 5, 116

Gurin, P. A., 5, 122

Gutman, A., 4, 116

H

Hawley, W. D., 113

Haycock, K., 30, 116

Hebert, J. M., 76, 118

higher education. *See* education: higher

Higher Education Opportunity Act of 1965 (HEA), 24, 31-32, 57

Higher Learning Commission of the North Central Association of Schools and Colleges (HLC), vi, 61-62

Hirsh, E. D., 53, 116

Hulten, C., 122

human rights, ix-x, 6, 22, 35, 59-60, 72, 74, 89, 91, 100, 104, 109

I

Infovillages.com, 40

Internationalization, 3, 9, 18, 22-23, 30, 45, 90, 92, 99, 104-105, 108

Irvine, J. J., 113

Iwata, K., 7, 100, 117

J

Jacoby, B., 102, 117

Johnson, D. W., 53, 117

Johnson, L., viii, 123

Johnson, R. T., 53, 117

justice (injustice), 5-6, 91

social, 36, 49, 55, 58, 69, 79, 82, 86-87, 104

K

K-12

curriculum, 55

educators, 57, 85

schools, x, 55, 61, 66, 69-70, 83, 109

students, 61, 70

teachers, 3, 55

youth, vii

Kogler, H., 103, 117

L

Larson, C. L., 53, 117

Layer, G., 4, 117

leaders, global. *See* global: leaders

LeBert, L., 115

Leder, S., 115

Levy, F., 17, 112

Levy, J., 53, 117

Lifelong learning, 30

Lorenz, D., 40, 117

Lyon, S., 53, 121

M

macroculture, 76, 78, 82

Mann, S., 90-92, 100, 121

Marginson, S., 51, 118

Mayer, J. D., 103, 122

McClelland, A., 115

McGee, C. A., 113

McIntyre, D. J., 53, 119

McNergney, R. F., 76, 118

"melting pot", 75, 77

Merryfield, M. M., 21, 118

Mesa-Bains, H., 53, 72, 121

Mesaric, T. C., 72, 98, 122

microculture, 56, 76, 78, 81-82

multicultural competence, 68, 82, 86, 88-89

Mundy, M., 115

Murnane, R. J., 17, 112

MySpace, 36, 40

N

National Association of Independent Colleges and Universities (NAICU), 33

National Committee for the Accreditation of Teacher Education (NCATE), vi, 60-61

Nieto, S., 58, 79, 86-87, 113, 118

O

Olsen, C. L., 22, 98, 100, 104, 118

Olson, N., 122

Ottoman, S., 118

outsource(-ing), ix, 18-20, 100

Ovando, C. J., 53, 117

P

Pang, V. O., 119

Perlman, J., 4, 119

perspectives

assimilation, 64, 74-78, 80, 89, 98

global, vii, ix-x, 3-8, 10, 13, 15, 18, 20-24, 28, 33, 45, 49-51, 59-60, 67-69, 73, 79, 81-83, 86, 88-89, 91-93, 95, 97-102, 104-105, 107-108

pluriversity, 9-11, 13, 104, 106, 108

Progress in International Reading Literacy Study (PIRLS), 70

Q

Quicksey, A., 36, 38, 119

Quin-Hilliard, D. B., 3, 103, 118

Quiseberry, N. L., 53, 119

R

Rhoads, R. A., 10, 35, 98, 119

Rubin, J., 40, 98, 120

S

Sacks, D. O., 120

Safford, P., 115

Sanderson, J., 18, 100, 120

Scott, M., 17, 120

shared culture. *See* cultures: shared culture

Shaw, S. M., 23, 67, 93, 120

Shenker, O., 67, 121

Sheil, C., 91, 121

Shiel, C., 67, 90, 92, 100-101, 106, 121

Shoenberg, R. F., 100, 118

Short, D., 5, 121

Shulman, J., 53, 121

Silverman, R., 53, 121

Slaughter, J. B., viii, 7, 121

Sleeter, C. E., 69, 121

Smith, D. G., 2, 4, 5, 7, 98, 122

Solovey, P., 103, 122

Southern Association of Colleges and Schools (SACS), vi, 62

South Korea, 21

STEM (Science, Technology, Engineering and Mathematics), vii, 17, 23-24, 93, 95, 104

Stephan, W. G., 113

Stueber, K., 103, 117

Suarez-Orozco, M. M., 3, 103, 118

Sumida, S., 5, 122

Szelenyi, K., 10, 35, 51, 98, 119

T

Thiel, P. A., 3, 21, 79, 98, 120

Thompson, D., 4, 116

tipping point, 16

Trends in International Mathematics and Science Study (TIMSS), 21, 70

Twitter, 36-37, 40

Twitty, J. R., 72, 98, 122

U

United States Census Bureau, 4, 71

U.S. Department of Education, 4, 24, 26, 30-32, 101, 108

"us-versus-them", 51

V

van Ark, B., 18, 122

W

Wang, H., 98, 122

Waters, M. C., 4, 119

Welty, W., 53, 121

Western Association of Colleges (WASC), 63

White, S., viii, 123

Wiles, J., 86, 123

Williams, A., 91, 121

Woock, C., 122